T0159040

SO YOU WANT TO BE A
COUNSELOR?

Frederick Fell Publishers, Inc
2131 Hollywood Blvd., Suite 305
Hollywood, Fl 33020
www.Fellpub.com
email: Fellpub@aol.com

Frederick Fell Publishers, Inc
2131 Hollywood Blvd., Suite 305
Hollywood, Fl 33020

For information about special discounts for bulk purchases, Please contact Frederick Fell Special Sales at business@fellpub.com.

Designed by Elena Solis

Manufactured in the United States of America

10 9 8 7 6 5 4 3 2 1

Library of Congress Cataloging-in-Publication Data

Nefer, Barbara, 1964-
So you want to be a counselor? / by Barbara Nefer.
    p. cm.
ISBN 978-0-88391-179-2 (pbk.)
1. Counseling--Vocational guidance. I. Title.
BF636.64.N44 2009
361'.0602373--dc22
                                        2009016145

ISBN 13: 978-0-88391-179-2

SO YOU WANT TO BE A COUNSELOR?

- Personal Insights from Professionals Working in the Field

- Information for Adult Students

- The Emerging Field of Online Counseling

- Online Schools —the Right Choice?

- What You Can Expect on the Job

- Getting Your License

- Companion Website with Updates

BARBARA NEFER

Dedication

To my husband, Tony, who stood by me through years of college and the crazy maze of licensure and continues to support me in my literary endeavors.

Acknowledgments

Acknowledgments go out to the Celebration Writers Group, especially Jan, Isabel and Charles, for their ongoing support of my work.

I also owe a debt of gratitude to the Absolute Write forums and the helpful individuals who populate them.

Thanks to "Help A Reporter Out" for linking me up with professionals who were willing to share their personal stories for this book and to my colleagues at LivePerson who added their experiences. A big thank-you to Patricia Berliner, Ph.D., Sue Carberry, Jason Fierstein, LPC, Kathleen Finnegan, LPC, Rev. Stephanie Florman, Sara Holliday, MFT, Rhonda Loft, LMFT, Sarah Maurer, Renee Murphy Hughes, LPC, Nancy Razza, Ph.D., Mary Robbins, LCSW, Dr. Ankur Saraiya, M. D., Jed Shlackman, LMHC, and Nancy Williams, LPC.

Also, I am grateful to Stitch, Farquaad, and Toonces, my three furry muses, who kept me company during long hours at the laptop.

NBCC information reprinted with the permission of the National Board for Certified Counselors, IncTM and Affiliates; 3 Terrace Way, Greensboro, NC 27403-3663.

Disclaimer

The insights and suggestions in this book are based on professional experience and research. The author, publisher, and other contributors will not bear any responsibility for liability, loss, or risk, personal or otherwise, that is incurred as a direct or indirect consequence of using or applying any of the information in this book. None of the information in this book should be viewed as legal or professional advice.

Examples in this book are not based on specific individuals. They are composites of many persons and situations. Names have been arbitrarily assigned.

Professional regulations, laws, ethical standards, academic requirements and other information related to professional counseling can change at any time. Always consult appropriate resources for the most current information.

Table of contents

Introduction

So You Want To Be A Counselor? is a definitive guide for anyone who is considering professional counseling as a career, from high school students up through adults of any age. This book covers general mental health counseling, as well as the most common specialized areas. It also takes an in-depth look at the rapidly evolving field of online therapy and discusses career options in related fields.

This book is written by a mental health counselor who practices both in person and online. It provides all of the information you'll need to make an informed decision on whether counseling might be the right job for you. It covers the required skills, personality traits, and investment in time, effort and money. It walks you through the complete process of pursuing a counseling career, from college preparation to choosing the right master's program, to navigating the state licensure maze and finding a permanent position. It also discusses the challenges and gives you a sample of what you'll experience on the job. It discusses the possibility of discovering that you've made the wrong choice and explores other career options that you can pursue with a counseling degree. When you're done reading So You Want To Be A Counselor?, you'll have everything you need to decide whether this is the right career for you.

UNIQUE FEATURES

This book has many unique features to help you with self-assessment and guide you to the most current information in rapidly changing areas. These features include:

- Website addresses where you can find up-to-date information on school accreditation, state licensing requirements, ethics, professional organizations, salaries, job searches, financial aid, and much more.
- Discussion of the evolving field of online counseling.
- An overview of related fields, such as psychiatry, social work, art and music therapy, and life coaching.
- Tips on choosing a legitimate online school as an alternative to a traditional bricks-and-mortar university.
- Special considerations for adults returning to school or considering college for the first time.
- Discussion of the personal investment it takes to become a counselor and the downsides of this field.
- Personal insights from the author, based on her own journey as an adult student pursuing a counseling career, and from other professionals in the mental health field.
- A companion blog at http://counselorwannabe.blogspot.com where you can find updated links and ask the author specific questions.

WHY YOU NEED THIS BOOK

According to the U. S. Department of Labor, Bureau of Labor Statistics (BLS), the field of professional counseling is poised for tremendous growth over the next several years. Once it was taboo to seek outside help, but the dwindling availability of personal support is rapidly changing this attitude. The number of people who say they have no one to discuss important issues with tripled between 1985 and 2004 (McPherson, Smith-Lovin, & Brashears, 2006). As people feel increasingly disconnected from personal support systems, they are turning to professionals to fill the void.

Because of this trend, talking to mental health professionals has become acceptable and even commonplace. Some laud it as a sign of strength because it shows that a person is willing to admit needing help and ask for it from an appropriate source. Talk shows and other popular media are reinforcing the importance of confronting issues, working through them, and using counselors as a catalyst to do so.

If you're mulling the possibility of pursing a counseling career, these growing opportunities mean that now is the perfect time to give it some serious consideration. You'll be entering a growing field where the demand for services is increasing steadily, along with the respect afforded to trained professionals.

WHO CAN USE THIS BOOK

This book is aimed at anyone, of any age and background, who is interested in becoming a professional counselor. This includes people in the following categories:

- Current high school students with an interest in psychology and related careers
- Undergraduate college students considering the counseling field
- Adults who are contemplating entering or re-entering the job market after an absence
- Adults who are currently working but who wish to embark on a new career path
- Anyone who is interested in what it takes to become a professional counselor

Choosing the right career is always important, but this is especially true when you're considering a field that takes a significant investment in time, money and effort. Because professional counseling requires a master's degree, practicum/internship, and completion of a licensure process, the decision to enter this field should not be made lightly.

If you think you'd like to become a mental health professional, this book will give you all the information you need to make an informed decision. If you choose to proceed, it will also guide you through the necessary steps to turn that choice into reality. Hopefully it will prove to be a valuable resource through the decision process and on through the journey of turning a spark of desire into the reality of a rewarding career.

NOTE

Throughout this book, there will be many references to mental health professionals and their clients. Statistics indicate that the majority of counselors are women, so female pronouns will be used to refer to counselors and other service providers and male pronouns will be used to refer to clients except in gender-specific examples. This is being done to maintain a consistent pattern and increase readability. It is not meant to exclude the males who have an interest in this field.

How this Book is Organized

This book is organized sequentially, starting off with information that will help you decide whether you really want to pursue a career in mental health counseling. This leads into what you can expect once you accept the commitment, including how to choose a school, what it will be like to attend college and earn your degree, and what you'll experience during the licensure process. It includes a discussion of how to find a job, what you can expect during a typical day as a mental health counselor, and common tools you might use. At the end, it explores the possibility of making the wrong choice and other ways you can use a counseling degree if you choose to leave the field. It concludes with a list of websites that provide current information on many of the topics discussed throughout the book.

Part One: Is Counseling the Right Career for You?

Part One of this book is designed to help you decide whether professional counseling is the best career choice for you. It explains what professional counselors do and discusses several similar professions. It also guides you through personal introspection that will help you decide whether counseling is the right choice or whether you might be more suited to a related career.

Chapter One: Why Do You Want to be a Counselor?

Chapter One gives an in-depth definition of professional counseling that goes beyond the dictionary and into practical applications. It discusses a counselor's role and the necessary traits for success in this field. It also explores ethical responsibilities and what a client should be able to expect from a mental health professional. This chapter will lead you through an exploration of your personal motivations. It poses several questions that will help you decide whether you have what it takes to be a counselor and whether you're considering this career for the right reasons.

Chapter Two: Common Counseling Professions

Chapter Two focuses on the specific job duties of several types of professional counselors. It covers school counselors, vocational counselors, rehabilitation counselors, mental health counselors, marriage and family therapists, and substance abuse counselors. You'll read about their duties, work environment, expected growth in the field, and earning potential. You'll also find personal insights from counselors currently working in each of these areas.

In this chapter you'll also learn about smaller but growing fields such as gerontological and genetic counseling that you might wish to consider.

Chapter Three: Therapeutic Specialties

Chapter Three covers specialized therapy and working with specific populations. It describes various fields such as sex therapy, play therapy, and other therapeutic approaches that are based on forms of artistic expression. These include art, music, dance, drama and poetry/literature. You'll learn about the additional training required for these specialties and how to become a certified practitioner through the appropriate professional organizations.

Chapter Four: Online Counseling

Chapter Four focuses on the rapidly expanding field of online counseling, both as a complement to a traditional counseling position and a stand-alone occupation. You will learn about the effectiveness of e-therapy, its potential benefits and drawbacks, and special ethical considerations for online practitioners.

Chapter Five: Salary and Long-Term Outlook for Professional Counselors

Chapter Five provides in-depth information on the current and long-term outlook for professional counseling jobs. Using U. S. Department of Labor statistics, it lays out salaries and projected growth through the year 2016. You'll also learn about the regional differences that can greatly affect your earning potential and how you can choose a field and employer to maximize your salary.

Chapter Six: Similar Professions

Chapter Six explores several fields that are similar to professional counseling. It gives full descriptions of each, including the training and education required and their earning potential, and poses several questions to help you determine your interest level. You'll learn about psychiatry, psychotherapy, psychiatric/mental health nursing. social work, pastoral counseling, and life coaching. This chapter also touches on the field of holistic counseling.

Chapter Seven: Are You Willing to Make the Investment?

Chapter Seven spells out the investment in time, money, education and effort that is required to become a mental health counselor. It covers the cost of schooling and various financial aid options. It lays out the time required for earning your degree and completing the licensure process. It presents information to help you decide whether you're ready to make the commitment that preparing for this career choice entails.

Chapter Eight: Special Challenges for Adults

Chapter Eight discusses the special challenges faced by adults returning to college or tackling it for the first time. It covers the time commitment, the challenge of juggling work and family responsibilities, and barriers to qualifying for scholarships and other types of financial aid.

This chapter also lists the ways in which many colleges and universities are smoothing the path for adult learners, including accelerated programs, flexible schedules, counseling, and support. It discusses the option of earning a degree online and how this can be especially beneficial for older students.

Chapter Nine: The Downside of Being a Counselor

Chapter Nine takes a realistic look at the downside of being a counselor. It spotlights many challenges you might face, such as dealing with difficult clients, handling the loss of a client to suicide, complying with mandated reporting laws, and working with insurance companies. It also discusses workplace violence, the risk of lawsuits and the importance of carrying professional liability insurance.

Part Two: The Nuts and Bolts of Becoming a Counselor

Part Two is for readers who believe that mental health counseling is indeed the right career choice. If you're confident and ready to proceed, it will give you all the information you need to become a counselor. You'll learn how to find an appropriate school and degree program, gain the necessary experience, achieve and maintain state licensure, and get a job in the professional counseling field. You'll also discover other ways you can use a counseling degree if you decide to change careers.

Chapter Ten: Your Education

Chapter Ten explains how to find an accredited school, either traditional or online, and gives a preview of the types of classes that are typically required to earn a graduate degree in counseling. It also gives warnings on how to recognize and avoid diploma mills that issue worthless degrees. This chapter explains the difference between school and program accreditation and why they are equally important. It discusses what you can expect in a typical mental health counseling curriculum.

Chapter Eleven: The Licensure Process

Chapter Eleven discusses the state licensure process. Virtually every state and the District of Columbia has licensing requirements for counseling professionals. This chapter gives a general overview of what these requirements entail and provides links to each state agency. You'll be able to find the specifics for your state and get the most up-to-date information on the appropriate website.

You'll also get a walk-through of the licensing process in an example state. This will cover the application; education and experience requirements; supervision; required examination; and continuing education to maintain your license. This chapter also covers the evolving topic of portability of counseling credentials for professionals who may wish to move to another state later in their career.

Chapter Twelve: Your Job Search

Chapter Twelve discusses the job search that you'll face once you're gotten your license. It covers typical ways to find leads and how to avoid scams. You'll learn about the main tools for your search, including a resume, cover letter, and references. This chapter alerts you to special mental health-related questions that you should be prepared to answer when you're called in for an interview. It also gives pointers on assessing a job offer and negotiating details that might not be satisfactory.

Chapter Thirteen: Working as a Mental Health Counselor

Chapter Thirteen discusses the importance of peer support for people working in the mental health field. It also covers tools of the trade often used by counselors, such as tests, assessments, and treatment planning books, and the advantages of joining a professional organization.

This chapter talks about what to expect in a first appointment with a prospective client. It also follows a professional counselor through a typical workday at a social service agency so you'll know what you might encounter on the job.

Chapter Fourteen: "Oh, No, I Made a Mistake!"

Chapter Fourteen addresses the dilemma you might face if you go through the entire process of becoming a counselor, only to discover that it's not the right job for you after all. It helps you evaluate whether you really want to leave the field or whether you can take power over the problem in another way.

This chapter discusses other jobs for which you would be qualified with a master's degree in counseling. These include human resources, education and training, criminal justice, management and supervision, and sales. It also covers ways in which you might meld counseling skills with personal interests, including fitness and writing, and turn them into a career. It covers volunteer opportunities that may allow you to do counseling on your own terms while working in another field.

Resources

The Resources section puts a comprehensive list of websites right at your fingertips. You'll be able to find the most up-to-date information about many of the topics covered in the book. It has a list of links to professional organizations, accreditation and quality assurance organizations, organizations and associations for related careers, codes of ethics, financial aid resources for college, and several places to find the most current job outlook and salary information and search for employment. Because internet links are subject to change, it also provides a blog link where you can find regular updates from the author.

Personal Insights

Throughout this book you'll find short anecdotes from the author and other mental health professionals. These will show you how the factual material in each chapter translates into the real world. You'll get a quick sampling of what you may experience as a counselor and how working professionals feel about various aspects of their jobs.

PART ONE

Is Counseling the Right Career for You?

Why Do You Want to be a Counselor?

Have you always been the person your friends come to for advice or a shoulder to cry on?

In a conflict, are you usually the peacemaker?

Do you have a special skill for guiding others to a compromise?

Are you able to reserve judgment and listen to all sides of an issue without interrupting to inject your own opinion?

Do you take a creative approach to problem-solving?

Do you think you would enjoy making a living by helping others work through their issues to reach their full potential?

If you answered yes to most or all of these questions, some form of professional counseling might be the perfect career for you. You've already got the traits and raw ability. Now you must be willing to invest the time, money and effort necessary to mold them into something useful. You'll need to go through the required schooling, internship and licensing process if you really want to turn your talents into a fulfilling profession.

A COUNSELOR'S ROLE

Contrary to popular belief, counselors don't fix people, give them specific advice, or tell them how to solve their problems. If you tend to be strong-willed and like to dictate solutions to others, you'll have to be able to let go of that when you're working in a professional capacity.

Most people have the ability to resolve their own issues or make the right choices. They simply need the proper tools and guidance to do so. A good counselor provides resources, nudges clients along, and helps them discover their own insights. Clients then use their new skills to resolve the problem that led them to seek help. As a bonus, they can apply this knowledge to future situations.

Mental Health and Hardware

To get an idea of the professional counselor's role, imagine someone in an empty room with a nail sticking out of the wall. His task is to pound the nail all the way into the wall. He probably has the physical capability to do it, but without a tool he's helpless. He can't pound it in with his fist, and he'd probably hurt himself if he tried. If you walk in, give him a hammer, and teach him how to use it properly, he is now equipped to accomplish the task. He can also use the same hammer to pound in any other nails he might encounter.

A counselor gives her clients a "hammer" in the form of exercises, cognitive tools, and insights gained simply through talking. She teaches them how to use their new tool to pound existing "nails" in their lives and take care of any others that might pop up in the future.

A Counselor's Focus

Some of the issues that a counselor might address are focused around common life challenges. For example, she might help clients manage anger or stress or support them in building self esteem or setting boundaries. Other issues might be more complex. Some clients may be struggling with serious mental health issues such as major depression, mood swings, or compulsions. In this case, the counselor's role would be supportive, and her goals would be aimed at helping the client manage his symptoms and minimize the impact of the disorder on his everyday life. She might even do family sessions to help other members learn how to provide healthy support while maintaining their own boundaries.

In these more serious cases, a counselor usually works in partnership with other mental health professionals. For example, a client with severe mood swings might see a psychiatrist to manage his medication. This medical treatment would be combined with regular visits to a counselor. In his sessions he would learn cognitive coping skills to help him manage the disorder's effects on his day-to-day functioning.

Contrary to popular belief, counselors don't fix people, give them specific advice, or tell them how to solve their problems.

24

WHAT IS PROFESSIONAL COUNSELING?

In a professional sense, counseling is often confused with the in-depth psychotherapy performed by a clinical psychologist or psychotherapist. When someone who isn't clear on the difference visualizes a counseling session, he often imagines a patient sprawled on a couch discussing their childhood traumas with a bespectacled, pipe-smoking sage. It's the old stereotype of Freudian psychoanalysis, which is actually much less common in today's world of Health Maintenance Organizations (HMOs) and managed care. In the present health care climate, insurers demand fast results rather than months and years of treatment.

The relationship between a professional counselor and her clients is on a more equal footing than what might be present when doing long-term psychotherapy. Counseling is focused more heavily on the present than the past, and it works toward life changes rather than simply trying to gain insight on past events. Psychotherapy often extends over a period of months, or even years, while counseling is typically short-term and aimed at providing tools that can be used immediately for change.

On average, counseling might run from six to twelve sessions, although it can extend for a longer period of time. Sessions take place on a weekly, bi-weekly or monthly basis, depending on the client's needs. If a counselor practices brief therapy, there might only be one or two sessions aimed at creating a targeted plan for a very specific issue.

Psychotherapy and counseling can be compared to traditional surgery vs. a laser procedure. Removing a growth surgically requires cutting out a larger area than a sharply focused laser beam. Both methods are effective, and both have their place in the medical field, but the laser is faster and only affects a clearly-defined area.

So What's the Difference?

Counselors are often confused with other mental health professionals, such as psychiatrists, psychologists, social workers, and even life coaches, who perform similar work. The differences will be covered in depth later in this book, but here is a quick summary of some of the most commonly confused areas:

• **Counselors cannot prescribe medication.** Psychiatrists are medical doctors, so they are able to prescribe psychotropic drugs and other medications. Depending on their practice location, some psychologists are also able to prescribe if they've had the proper training.

When someone who isn't clear on the difference visualizes a counseling session, they often imagine a patient sprawled on a couch discussing their childhood traumas with a bespectacled, pipe-smoking sage.

•*Most counselors are not "doctors."* A mental health counseling license typically requires a master's degree, so that is what most counselors have. They can go on to earn a doctorate degree in psychology or any other topic, which would make them a doctor of psychology or whatever academic subject they've chosen. These are **Ph.D.** degrees, meaning "doctor of philosophy," not **M.D.** degrees, which indicate "medical doctor." On its own, a doctorate doesn't grant the holder the right to legally practice counseling. Licensure is still required.

•*In most states, "counselor" is a licensed title, and psychologists, social workers, and other professionals are not legally "counselors."* While the exact title varies, most states require anyone who calls herself a counselor to meet specific educational and experiential requirements and to have a valid license. While psychologists and social workers may do similar work, their professions have their own requirements for licensure and their own legal titles.

Some related fields, such as life coaching, do not currently have licensure requirements, although certification is available from professional organizations. People working in these unlicensed fields cannot legally call themselves "counselors" or advertise their work as "counseling" in states that regulate those terms.

CHARACTERISTICS OF PROFESSIONAL COUNSELING

While the word "counseling" is a general term that can be used to describe various forms of providing support and guidance to others, professional mental health counseling is a specific career choice. Individuals who pursue it must prepare by following a clearly defined set of requirements for education and licensure. Then they'll take on a prescribed role with clients, working with them in a structured manner and following a set of ethical standards.

Preparation

Practitioners must take a specific course of study and earn a graduate degree in counseling or a closely related field. In order to be called a "professional counselor," "therapist," or related job title, virtually every state requires a person to obtain a license that is contingent on meeting certain educational and experiential requirements. To maintain this license, the counselor is required to follow the ethics and standards set out by the appropriate licensing board and obtain continuing education credits as specified by her state. She may also choose to join a professional organization that provides resources and networking and abide by their ethics and quality of care standards. National certification is another voluntary option.

Role With Clients

Although she doesn't tell people what to do, a counselor takes an active role when dealing with her clients. Rather than listening passively and offering no feedback, she encourages them to talk and helps them find insights in the conversation. She provides a safe environment for venting and a place where people can speak without judgment, and she also helps clients find wisdom in their own words. This becomes the basis of showing them how take power and implement personal, positive change.

For example, a counselor might be working with a client who feels that his mother-in-law is meddling in his marriage. He may need to vent his frustration, and the counselor listens and makes neutral comments. She doesn't judge him in any way, like saying, "You're being too harsh!" or "Your mother-in-law is good to your children. You should just put up with it and be grateful that she cares." No matter what she thinks personally, she only gives objective responses.

Once he's done, she helps him isolate the specific problems that need resolution. He may feel that his mother-in-law is undermining his disciplinary efforts with his children and that she is being rude by visiting several evenings each week without calling first. These are concrete behaviors that are fueling his stress, anger and frustration. Now the counselor can help him set the emotion aside and focus his energy on making changes. They might discuss how to impose and maintain boundaries where the children are concerned, how to implement and enforce rules for visits, and how to get his spouse to support these efforts.

The counselor finds ways to empower her clients and help them become actors rather than simply reacting to their issues and environment. Whether she is working as a general mental health counselor or in a particular specialty, her ultimate goal is to teach people how to tap into their own power and take control of their lives through active choice-making.

Among the various counseling specialties, the main difference is in the specific area where empowerment is sought. It might be in the client's personal, family, educational or professional life or a combination of these areas. Thus he might choose to work with a mental health counselor, marital and family therapist, vocational counselor or other appropriate professional, depending on the situation.

Expertise

Because professional counseling encompasses so many areas, counselors only practice in those for which they have appropriate training, expertise, licensure and work experience. In addition to opting for a general mental health counseling practice, a counselor might choose from among many specialties such as school or vocational counseling, rehabilitation counseling, life stage transition issues, or marital and family therapy.

Some of these specialties require additional coursework before a counselor can be licensed. For example, many states impose additional education-related requirements on school counselors or require additional graduate classes for marriage and family therapists. For other professional concentrations, even if there are no formal requirements, a counselor may gain on-the-job experience and join appropriate professional organizations for information, networking and support. She can also attend seminars and continuing education classes to expand her knowledge. She may even be able to find an experienced mentor who will offer personalized guidance.

As an example, a counseling student named Mitch wanted to work with gay and lesbian clients. While his school had no specific degree concentration in this area, he took as many electives as possible related to diversity and social issues. Because he was a student member of the American Counseling Association (ACA), he was able to join the Association for Lesbian, Gay, Bisexual & Transgender Issues in Counseling (ALGBTIC), an ACA division focused on eliminating prejudice and providing a safe counseling environment for this population. He joined the ALGBTIC mentoring program and served his practicum and internship at a clinic offering counseling specifically for gay and lesbian clients. Even though he earned a general mental health counseling degree, Mitch felt that these other activities provided him with the expertise to specialize in gay and lesbian issues in his work.

Population Served

Professional counselors generally work with clients who are functioning within a normal range in their daily lives, even though there may be some problems. These clients are usually dealing with adjustment issues, emotional turmoil, or situational concerns which can usually be resolved within weeks or months. Unless they're working in an inpatient facility or similar environment, most counselors don't deal with people who are struggling with active symptoms of a serious mental illness or severe impairment.

Most clients who seek out a professional counselor already have the knowledge they need and are simply looking for a way to tap into it, clarify it and get it validated by a neutral party before they are comfortable putting it to use. While a counselor might help a client manage the day-to-day effects of a mental health issue, she leaves assessment and diagnosis of specific mental disorders and management of medications in the hands of a psychiatrist or psychologist.

Structure

Professional counselors work within a structured setting and use theory-based interventions in their treatment of clients. They may focus on one particular therapeutic style or use a combination. Their relationship with a client moves through a prescribed set of stages, which normally includes the following:

• *The initial assessment session.* This gives the counselor a chance to determine the scope of the client's problem and whether it falls within her expertise to treat. It also allows the client to meet the counselor and get a sense of her personality and style. The counselor shares a basic description of her treatment philosophy and how she would approach the issue. The client then decides whether he wishes to proceed with regular sessions.

• *The work phase.* This is the meat of the counselor/client relationship. It is focused on taking concrete steps to move towards mutually established goals. The counselor creates a treatment plan and guides the client through it. If their work is successful, he learns new skills that he can use to handle the problematic issue and apply to other areas of his life, now and in the future.

• *Termination.* The sessions end at a mutually agreed upon point when the client has gained insight and is actively applying the tools he has learned and seeing positive changes. Ideally, he can also use them to head off future issues without the need to return to therapy. Even though the therapeutic relationship may have formally terminated, he can schedule a "brush up" session or two if needed.

Overall, the counselor's role is to guide clients into new, more effective ways of thinking, feeling and behaving. She does goal-based work that improves the client's overall functioning and empowers him to carry out the steps required to achieve resolution rather than sticking to old, ineffective patterns or reactions. Once this process is completed, her work comes to a logical conclusion.

Professional counselors use the specific techniques and tools that they learn about in their degree program. However they should still maintain the flexibility to adapt techniques and experiment with new ones if they believe that it's in a client's best interest. Sometimes a difficult problem might need a creative solution, so counselors must know when to follow their gut instincts and take a risk. Creativity has led to an expansion of counseling techniques, and many counselors now use art, music, poetry, literature, and even dance or drama in their work. You should always be open to exploring new approaches, as long as there is no potential to harm the client.

Personal Insight

Jed Shlackman, LMHC, a licensed mental health counselor practicing in Miami, FL, sees counseling as "offering guidance and resources to help people enhance their ability to handle life's challenges." He says, "This includes assisting people in understanding mental and emotional processes and finding healthy ways of perceiving things and managing emotions."

Jed defines effective counselors as those who are able to "build rapport and trust with their clients, gaining insight about the clients' beliefs and perceptions. Then, counselors can offer guidance and interventions to help people shift their own patterns of thinking and behaviors."

He says, "A major part of counseling is for the therapist or counselor to develop a connection and resonance with people who are receiving services, which allows for effective therapeutic communication to unfold. This communication occurs on multiple levels. It can be role modeling, conscious verbal input, subconscious guidance through trance states and environmental cues, or even bodywork psychotherapy.

"Flexibility and knowledge are both useful to help counselors connect with their clients and foster positive transformation, using whichever methods clients are receptive and responsive to."

TYPICAL TRAITS OF A COUNSELOR

Effective counselors tend to share some common traits that contribute to success in their profession. These include:

- Self respect and respect for others
- A healthy sense of self-esteem
- An optimistic outlook
- The ability to fully attend to another person and use active listening and other good communication skills
- The ability to model healthy behaviors
- A good sense of humor
- Compassion, empathy and caring
- Respect for diversity in all its forms
- Patience
- A non-judgmental attitude
- Creativity
- Flexibility
- The ability to reframe negative situations into positive learning opportunities

A counselor must also be secure in her own identity and want to enter a mental health profession for the right reasons.

A counselor must also be secure in her own identity and want to enter a mental health profession for the right reasons. If you get an esteem boost by "rescuing" other people, your motivation may not be healthy. It's normal to gain some satisfaction by helping others work through their issues, but this must

30

come in a depersonalized way. If you grew up in a dysfunctional household or have a troubled background, you may have an internal desire to fix others that is spurred by your efforts to fix your own situation. This will prevent you from being objective and keep you from helping your clients effectively.

You don't have to come from a perfect family to be a good counselor. Having some rough edges in your background can give you a genuine sense of empathy that many clients will sense and appreciate. You do need the ability to separate your own background and issues from your professional viewpoint and work. If you're serious about becoming a mental health counselor, you may benefit from going through some therapy sessions yourself. Not only will this give you a taste of what it feels like to be on the other side of the room, but it will also ensure that your motivations are healthy.

ETHICAL RESPONSIBILITIES

Because their work has a direct effect on their clients' lives and well-being, and by extension on their family and friends, counselors must abide by strict ethical guidelines that cover their professional conduct. These standards are laid out by state licensing boards. Many professional organizations, such as the American Counseling Association (ACA), have their own ethical code that members are expected to follow. At least 19 state boards have adopted the ACA's code for their state requirement. The National Board for Certified Counselors also has a code of ethics for those who have earned its certification.

Areas Typically Covered by Ethics

Even though different states and organizations may have their own ethical standards, there are several commonalities. These usually involve the protection of clients, including how a counselor interacts with them, both professionally and personally, and guards their privacy and well-being.

Client Welfare

Client welfare is one of the most important ethical considerations for a counselor. There is an implied sense of trust when someone opens up to his counselor, and she must make sure she is worthy of his faith. They may be discussing some very personal issues, so she must take special care to protect his well-being and to do the same for all of her clients. This can be accomplished by following professional standards; ensuring quality of care; creating an appropriate, customized treatment plan; keeping proper records; and involving the client's outside support network in the treatment process if appropriate.

An ethical counselor is also required to handle termination of services with care. Most counseling relationships come to a natural end. The counselor and client mutually agree that the goals have been achieved and the client is ready to move forward on his own.

Sometimes, however, a counselor might need to terminate a client for a variety of reasons. She might feel that he's not making progress or that they've reached an impasse and he might benefit from a different type of program. She might have to take a break from her practice or lighten her client load for an unavoidable reason. In any of these cases, she cannot simply "abandon" the client. Instead, she must assist him in finding and transitioning to a new professional who can offer appropriate treatment.

The decision to terminate a client for personal reasons should not be made lightly. It should only be a last resort if the counselor cannot resolve the issue through discussions with the client or consultations with her supervisor. If termination is necessary, it must be presented in a way that doesn't put blame on the client or make him feel that he said or did something wrong. The reasons should be discussed objectively, and the counselor should offer support in finding another professional. Otherwise he may lose faith in the "safety" of a therapeutic relationship.

For example, let's say that you're working at a social service agency, but you're planning to move to another town and will be taking a new job closer to home. You can't just toss up your hands and tell your clients, "In one month you're on your own!" You must help them find another counselor to continue their work or refer them to an appropriate program and do what you can to ensure a smooth transition.

For individual clients, you might refer them to other colleagues at the agency and perhaps even hold a joint session before you leave. For a family you've been working with on communication issues, you might refer them to a support group focused on listening skills and conflict resolution among family members. You haven't fulfilled your ethical responsibility until all of your service receivers have alternate arrangements in place.

Informed Consent

Clients often deal with sensitive issues in their counseling sessions and they expect their privacy to be respected. Counselors must strive to maintain this trust and create a safe environment. However there are circumstances in which a counselor must break confidentiality under mandated reporting laws. Reporting is typically required when the client is in imminent danger of committing suicide or has made a direct threat to someone else. Cases of child or elder abuse usually fall into this category too.

A counselor may also share information about a particular case with her supervisor. Supervision is an important way to ensure quality of care. To accomplish this, it requires discussion of clients, their issues, and the treatment plan. The information must be specific enough for the supervisor to be able to make suggestions and recommendations.

A professional counselor must fully disclose these exceptions to potential clients before they enter treatment. The prospective client then has the option of signing a form giving his informed consent or may opt not to go ahead with the counseling.

Disclosure to the client should include the ways in which the counselor will divulge information; the exact circumstances in which this might happen; the nature of what would be disclosed; why it would be done; and to whom it would be given.

Sometimes a counseling relationship will change. For example, a counselor might be working with an individual who decides to switch to couples therapy or requests sessions with other family members. If this happens, a new informed consent must be presented, discussed and signed so that all participants can show their agreement with the new arrangement.

Personal Relationships with Clients

Over the course of treatment, personal feelings might develop between a counselor and client. Sometimes these feelings go beyond simple friendship, and at an extreme they can lead to the mutual desire for an intimate relationship. This is problematic because clients are usually in an emotionally vulnerable position when they retain mental health services. They may not be in the right frame of mind to make a healthy decision about having intimate contact with someone in a position of authority.

Virtually every set of ethics forbids counselors from entering into sexual relationships with clients currently under their care. This prohibition typically extends to intimate relationships with members of a client's family too. Some codes allow such a relationship after the termination of treatment, but only within certain time restrictions. Normally a certain number of years must pass before a counselor and former client can ethically engage in intimate contact. Even when the allowable timeframe has passed, a counselor should exercise caution before choosing to become intimate with someone for whom she has provided treatment.

Let's say that you have a client to whom you really relate. He reminds you of a former boyfriend who really touched your heart. You also feel sorry for him because he's just come out of a rough relationship. His girlfriend dumped him abruptly and with no explanation, so he's still buried in grief. Even though you try to depersonalize, a little voice in your mind whispers, "Doesn't she realize how lucky she was to have him? If he were my boyfriend, I'd never hurt him like that." You're finding it harder and harder to remain objective.

As the therapeutic relationship progresses, you realize that your feelings have definitely moved beyond a professional level. You find yourself fantasizing about a romantic relationship. You sense that he might feel the same way because he's been acting flirtatious lately, and he gave you a lingering hug at the end of his last session that went beyond gratitude or friendship.

You must be able to recognize the danger signs in this situation and implement boundaries immediately. When the client brings up something personal or acts flirtatious, you must redirect him back to an appropriate topic. If he asks you outright about the possibility of a relationship, you must discuss the ethical implications and lay out the proper boundaries. If you're unsure of how to handle the situation, you should consult with your supervisor or a trusted colleague.

Intimate relationships aren't the only danger zone. Ethical guidelines also discourage counselors from entering into non-sexual friendships with clients and their family members outside of the professional relationship. However, some contact might be allowed if there is a potential benefit. For example, it might be appropriate for the counselor to attend a client's wedding, birthday party, or some other celebratory event. She might also be able to provide support during a difficult time, such as a funeral or court hearing for a divorce.

The decision to have contact with a client outside of the office should not be made lightly. If a counselor believes it is appropriate in a certain circumstance, she should thoroughly document the reasons for that choice and spell out her rationale of the benefits. If she has any doubts, she should discuss the situation with her supervisor or a colleague whose opinion she respects. She should also clearly explain the limited nature of the contact to the client.

Let's say you have a client who is having her first birthday party in nearly a decade. When she entered therapy, her birthday brought on depression and she refused to celebrate. Now she has conquered those feelings and is planning a huge bash. Because you helped guide her through her recovery, she really wants you to attend.

You consider the situation and decide that it would be a beneficial show of support to be there for her. You have a quick meeting with your supervisor to do a reality check and confirm that your rationale is sound. Then you document everything in the client's file, including the specific reasons why you think she will benefit from your presence and how it will support your therapeutic work. Before the party, you let her know that you are making an exception to your usual policy so she won't misunderstand, misread your actions, or build up unrealistic expectations.

Accepting Gifts From Clients

Due to the nature of the counseling relationship, clients might develop an emotional bond with a counselor similar in nature to how they would regard a trusted friend. This may include wanting to give a gift, either in observance of a holiday or simply out of feelings of friendship or gratitude. While this might seem like a natural gesture, counselors must exercise great caution in choosing to accept presents from clients. Even though emotional closeness might grow, it's still a professional relationship and needs to be maintained as such. Generally, a counselor should politely refuse anything other than a token item. The refusal must be done with care, and the counselor should explain the reasons. She can say that she's acting on ethical requirements rather than making a personal rejection.

For example, you may have a client who is grateful for your support during her very difficult divorce. In gratitude, she presents you with an expensive designer purse. You should explain that you are grateful for the gesture but that you are bound by professional ethics that forbid you from accepting. If the client pushes, you can say, "I appreciate your offer, but the ethical standards aren't optional. They are mandated by the state, and it could jeopardize my license if I don't follow them. I'm sure you can understand that I don't want to threaten my professional standing." This shifts the decision away from you and links it to an external, objective reason rather than a personal rejection.

What Clients Should Be Able To Expect

A client should be able to expect certain things from an ethical counselor. At the most basic level, their expectations should include the following:

- ***Counselors should share their qualifications and information about their specific areas of expertise with their clients.*** This should include license and certification information and any special classes, seminars or other education above and beyond the master's degree.
- ***Counselors should offer treatment to all clients, and treat them with respect.*** This should be done without regard for factors such as their age, sex, race, religion, marital status, sexual orientation, socioeconomic status, and disability.
- ***Counselors should inform clients about what the treatment process entails.*** This includes an explanation of how goals will be determined, the techniques that will be used, typical limitations of treatment, and the potential benefits and risks of the counseling process.
- ***Counselors should inform clients about confidentiality, privacy, and circumstances that would require disclosure of information.*** They should seek a client's signed acknowledgment that they have discussed this information and that the client consents to treatment.

- ***Counselors should clearly disclose the financial aspect before the counseling relationship begins.*** This should include the cost of each session and billing/collection policies.
- ***Counselors should assist client with making alternative arrangements for service if required.*** Circumstances in which this might be necessary include the counselor's temporary absence, permanent termination of services for an unavoidable reason, or the need for a referral for other services.

Resolving Ethical Dilemmas

When they run into a dilemma, counselors are required to resolve it within the scope of the relevant ethics. While specific guidelines are dictated by state licensing boards and professional organizations, the process usually resembles the following:

- ***Clarification of the situation.*** What is the exact ethical dilemma and the situation that is causing it? What is the question that must be answered or the decision to be made? Lay out the specifics of the dilemma and the type of action that will ultimately be required.
- Consideration of who will be affected by this decision. While ethical dilemmas generally arise as the result of a situation with a particular client, their effects can have a much wider impact. Consider the ripple effect on others with whom the client interacts, including family members, friends, and co-workers. Ask yourself, could it affect other clients under your care or your co-workers and peers?
- ***Consideration of your knowledge and experience level.*** Are you equipped to make this decision? Have you ever faced a similar situation in the past? If not, are there others with more experience who could give you guidance? Make a list of everyone whom you might be able to tap for their input.
- ***Consultation of resources on professional ethics.*** Virtually every state requires licensed counselors to abide by a specified code of ethics. Many professional organizations also have their own codes for members. Refresh yourself on this material, and use it to guide your decisions. Consult as many codes as you can find and look for trends and similarities.
- ***Consideration of legal ramifications.*** Are there certain requirements spelled out in the law for handling this type of situation? Could your decision have possible legal repercussions? If you're not sure about this aspect, you should consult an attorney for guidance. Find one who has special expertise in the area of professional counseling and the mental health field. You may be able to get a referral from a colleague or professional organization.

- ***Exploration of other resources.*** There may be literature, studies and other resources that lay out facts or discuss similar situations. This could give you information to consider or inform you about precedents in handling this sort of dilemma. Search professional journals and any online resources that may be available through professional organizations. If you don't have access to journals, visit a local university library.
- ***Consideration of the influence of your emotional feelings.*** If the situation is a particularly difficult or emotionally charged one, your own feelings and biases might cloud your objectivity. Depending on what is at stake, your personal interest might come into play too. Focus on how you can back away from all those factors and consider the situation objectively. You may need to do an objective reality test. If you can't do it yourself, get an unbiased review from your supervisor or another professional who has no stake in the matter.
- ***Consideration of the outcome and impact of each possible decision.*** In your mind, play out the scenario that would be most likely to occur for each course of action. Put yourself in the role of each person who might be affected and try to have empathy for their feelings. This will force you to consider the ripple effect and the potential aftermath of each possible decision.
- ***Asking for outside help.*** Outside experts can assist when you might not have enough knowledge or experience to make an informed decision. They may even have direct experience if they've ever been through a similar situation, and if you're consulting more than one person you might notice a trend. While you don't necessary have to handle your dilemma in the recommended way, it will give you some solid information to consider when making your own decision.
- ***Being prepared to take responsibility for your decision.*** Know the basis by which you arrived at your choice and be comfortable with your entire decision process. Don't leave any room for second guessing. You should also be prepared to handle any consequences or fallout that occurs as a result of your decision.
- ***Making use of the knowledge gained.*** When you've faced a difficult ethical dilemma, you end up gaining valuable experience just by going through the decision process, following through with an action plan, and dealing with the end result. Whether it's a positive or negative outcome, you'll still gain valuable insight. Use it to guide your own future decisions and to assist colleagues with similar dilemmas.

Ethics Complaints

If a client has a concern or feels that you've committed an ethical violation, you must be fully prepared to address that concern openly and objectively.

The client should be able to bring up any topic with you and expect you to handle it professionally. You should listen to his concern and try to find an acceptable solution. It might be appropriate to involve your supervisor in the discussion if both you and the client agree.

If a client isn't satisfied after discussing the issue with you and/or your supervisor, or if he isn't comfortable bringing it up with you, he can report his concerns to the appropriate state agency. They will typically investigate the allegations and give you a chance to present your side. If the agency feels that the charges have merit, they may impose sanctions against you. This can include anything from a warning to revoking your license temporarily or permanently, depending on the seriousness of the breach and whether you've committed other ethical violations in the past.

If you are a member of the American Counseling Association (ACA) or any other professional organization that requires adherence to a code of ethics, or if you are certified by the National Board for Certified Counselors (NBCC), your clients can also file complaints with these organizations.

Where to Find More Information

The information presented in this section is very general. It covers some of the most common points that are typically included in mental health-related codes of ethics. You can get specific information by contacting your state's licensure board to request a copy of the code they use. You can also review the ethical codes adhered to by members of various professional organizations for counselors. These are often available for review even if you are not a member yourself.

You can find the ACA's code of ethics, which is used by many state boards, on their website at www.counseling.org/Resources/CodeOfEthics/TP/Home/CT2.aspx. The code of ethics for the NBCC is posted on their website at www.nbcc.org/AssetManagerFiles/ethics/nbcc-codeofethics.pdf.

FIVE CRITICAL QUESTIONS

If you're seriously considering professional counseling as a career, you'll need to possess the traits discussed in this chapter and be able to incorporate them into your interactions with clients. You'll also have to be willing to abide by the appropriate ethical standards. Almost any college student can learn theories of counseling and understand how they are implemented on an objective level. That's not enough to be an effective counselor. You have to be able to translate that knowledge into positive, healthy interactions with clients.

The following five questions will help you determine whether you possess the core skills and abilities that can be molded and developed into a successful career in professional mental health counseling. If you can't honestly answer "yes" to each of these critical questions, you'll need to do some personal work before choosing the counseling field.

1) Could you unconditionally support your clients even when their views are in direct contrast to your own? For example, let's say that you personally have a strong opposition to abortion. A client is facing an unplanned pregnancy and wants you to lead her through an objective reality test to help her arrive at the best decision for her personal situation. Could you set aside your own beliefs and guide her to a purely objective decision? If not, are you willing to admit this and refer her to someone who can?

2) Do you have any biases and prejudices that might get in the way of treating certain populations? If so, can you overcome them? Professional counselors are encountering an increasingly diverse client base. This will continue to expand as online counseling gains popularity, allowing you to potentially work with clients anywhere in the world. Are you willing to work with people of all races, ethnicities and belief systems? Can you interact comfortably with gay and lesbian clients? What about those who are struggling with sexual addictions or fetishes? Are you willing to go through cultural sensitivity training to better prepare you for counseling groups with which you don't have much experience?

For example, let's say that you are an atheist and don't believe in the existence of God or any other higher power. You're working with a client who is exploring his sense of spirituality. Can you support him objectively, even if he feels that it's leading him to attend a church or explore a specific religion? If he asks about your personal beliefs, can you redirect him back to his own journey in a neutral way?

3) Will you be able to maintain your clients' confidentiality? One of the most important ethical duties of a counselor is to provide a safe environment and protect a client's privacy. With very few exceptions, everything that you discuss in a counseling session is confidential. You can't share it with your partner or laugh about it at lunch with your co-workers. Doing so is a serious ethical breach even if your client never finds out. If he somehow discovered that you weren't protecting his privacy, you'd be responsible for shattering his trust and the integrity of your professional relationship, as well as committing an ethical violation for which he could file a complaint.

In general, the only circumstances in which a counselor must break confidentiality are when a person is in danger of harming himself or someone else, if there is a disclosure of child or elder abuse, or if there is a court order. Other than these legally mandated circumstances, the only person with whom a counselor can share client information is her supervisor, and this is for the sole purpose of quality assurance and guidance. The supervisory process is disclosed to clients up front so they can provide informed consent.

For example, if you're at a party with some friends and they find out that you're a counselor, they might say, "Wow, you must hear some wild stuff!

What's the weirdest thing a client ever told you?" Will you be able to draw a firm boundary? If you say, "Ethically I can't talk about that" and they continue to press, can you maintain a firm refusal?

4) Will you be able detach from your clients? Even though you are a trained counselor, you're also a human being. You're not immune from feelings and the effects of your own past and present experiences, so certain clients and situations might push your buttons or hit you emotionally. For example, perhaps you're working with a client who confesses that he abused an animal. As a pet lover this disturbs you, but you can't let it color your professional relationship. You must remain non-judgmental, remove emotion from the equation, and maintain a safe environment for the client to continue sharing despite your personal upset.

As someone who is considering counseling as your profession, you probably have a strong tendency to nurture and care. Ironically, many people who are drawn to this career tend to have a deep sense of empathy, which puts them at greater risk for getting too emotionally close to a client's problems. It's hard not to let your heart go out to a battered woman, abused child, or other sympathetic clients. These emotions are natural, but if you let them take power over you, you'll quickly get bogged down. Your own life and relationships may even be affected because you're experiencing stress, anxiety or depression.

When you take your clients' problems on board to the point where they're draining you emotionally, you also lose the ability to give them effective care. You must make self-care and detachment a priority, not only for your own sake, but also for the people you serve. Find private ways to vent, such as journaling, or talk to your supervisor or peers as soon as you recognize the danger signs that you might be getting too involved in your work.

Some clients may project their own negative emotions onto you. This is actually a normal part of the therapeutic process. For example, you might be working with a young woman who has issues with her mother. During the course of your work together, you may take on a maternal role in her eyes. She may vent anger and frustration onto you as a safe substitute for her real mother. You have to recognize this as a healthy part of the process and be prepared to accept her venting and to deal with it in an objective manner, without taking it to heart.

When you take your clients' problems on board to the point where they're draining you emotionally, you also lose the ability to give them effective care.

Like physicians and police officers, counselors must be able to build and maintain a shell of detachment. They must keep their feelings in check in the workplace, deal with situations objectively, and know how to put the intense emotions aside instead of bringing them home. If you can't develop the appropriate self-protective skills, mental health counseling is probably not the right field for you because you'll most likely burn out early on.

5) Will you be able to deal with failure? Many freshly minted counselors leave school and venture out into their internships with visions of miraculously changing the world, one person at a time. Harsh reality soon sets in, as many counseling jobs have a relatively low success rate. This varies by your area of practice, but if you work in certain environments, such as a social service agency, substance abuse clinic or other program made up mainly of court-ordered participants or otherwise reluctant clients, you may quickly become disheartened by the number of people who relapse or simply drop out of treatment.

You might be the world's most skilled counselor, but you're bound by the old cliché that you can lead a horse to water but you can't make it drink. Many clients seek counseling because they are being pushed by a family member, friends, their boss, or even a judge. They don't believe that they need to change, so they might play along for a while but they won't really internalize the content of your sessions. The more you try to get them to actively participate, the more resistant they will become. To them, participation would mean an admission of fault, and their denial prevents them from taking any responsibility for their problems.

You will also have clients who sincerely want to improve their lives until they discover just how much work is involved. They may come to counseling expecting you to hand out easy solutions to their problems or tell them exactly what to do. Once they learn that you're simply a guide and that they have to do the bulk of the work and make their own decisions, they'll cancel their next appointment or simply never show up again.

You must learn to detach from negative outcomes. If you take every failure personally, you'll be buried in frustration and lose the ability to work effectively even when you're dealing with motivated clients. As long as you have a good supervisor who will keep your performance on track, remind yourself that you're helping people to the best of your ability and that you can't force them to respond. There will always be some clients who truly want to achieve success and are willing to do the work involved. When you're feeling discouraged, focus on your positive outcomes as a touchstone to keep an upbeat outlook.

 *Personal Insight*

FROM THE AUTHOR: When I was completing my practicum at a social service agency, I worked with a young man who entered counseling because of his girlfriend. He was one of my very first clients. He was having anger issues, and she told him that she'd break up with him if he didn't get some help. Even though he'd been pushed into treatment by an ultimatum, he recognized that he had a problem and was very motivated in our work.

We worked together for several months and he made some very positive changes. He had been acting out his anger in inappropriate ways. In counseling, he learned how to channel it into healthy outlets and he was able to implement this when interacting with his girlfriend. He also adapted this to other areas of his life, such as dealing with family members and co-workers.

Unfortunately his girlfriend ended up breaking up with him anyway. He was so distraught that he abruptly dropped out of counseling. This hit me really hard because he had been doing so well, and I feared that his grief might cause him to slip back into old behaviors. I never knew whether that happened or not, but it bothered me for a long time.

As I gained experience, I was able to detach from the situation and accept the fact that he was responsible for his own choices. I'd given him the tools, and he'd proven that he was capable of using them. But I couldn't force him to continue that use, and if I agonized over the outcome I'd block my effectiveness with other clients. It was a hard lesson but I'm glad that I learned it early on.

SO ARE YOU READY?

If you answered most or all of these questions with an emphatic "yes," you've taken the first step towards a career in professional counseling. While you must be prepared to go through years of schooling and gaining work experience, along with a rigorous licensing process, knowing that you have the necessary traits will help reassure you that those investments are truly worth it.

CHAPTER SUMMARY

- Professional counselors guide clients in examining their thoughts, emotions and behavior to help them make decisions and live life more effectively. They do not give direct advice. Instead, they help clients find their own insights and solutions.
- Counselors share certain traits that include empathy, patience, an upbeat and non-judgmental attitude, and a willingness and desire to help others.

- Counselors abide by a code of ethics dictated by the state in which they are licensed. If they belong to a professional organization, it may have its own code of ethics for members to follow.
- When faced with a tough dilemma, a counselor must consider the ethical implications before making a decision.
- Anyone who is seriously considering becoming a professional counselor must be prepared for some introspection. You must be able to support clients unconditionally, put aside personal prejudices, maintain confidentiality, detach from your clients' issues, avoid becoming emotionally involved, and deal with failure.

COMMON COUNSELING PROFESSIONS

Professional counseling is a broad term that refers to guiding others as they work through their problems, cope with cognitive, personal and emotional issues, and learn to make healthy decisions. At the most basic level, a mental health counselor develops an interpersonal helping relationship with her clients for the purpose of guiding them through an exploration of their thoughts, feelings and behaviors. This information is processed for insights which the client can use to make concrete changes and improvements in his life. The framework in which this is accomplished can vary widely, depending on where a counselor works, the therapeutic techniques she prefers to use, and the population she is serving.

Counselors can be found in a wide variety of settings, from schools to in-patient and out-patient mental health facilities to job training programs to rehabilitation centers. They may work with virtually any segment of the population, from children up through older adults. Their clients are often widely diverse in terms of race, religion, culture, and background. Typical groups they might treat include disabled clients, at-risk youngsters, aging adults, abused women, gay/lesbian individuals and couples, or just about anyone who may be in need of emotional assistance and support.

No matter what professional setting you prefer or which population you find most appealing as a client base, there is an area of counseling for you. Here are some of the most common fields:

SCHOOL COUNSELING
What Does a School Counselor Do?

School counselors may also be known as educational counselors, guidance counselors, or even vocational counselors if they're serving an older population. Their job duties are similar, no matter what the label. The main difference is usually based on the age group they're serving.

The overall purpose of a school counselor is to provide students with age-appropriate services that support a successful academic performance. For younger students, this involves supporting them in their school work and social problems that might affect it, as well as assessing and addressing any special needs. For older students, they also provide guidance as high schoolers approaching graduation prepare for college, trade school, or direct entry into the workforce.

School counselors may also teach life skills classes on topics such as stress management, study skills, and alcohol and drug awareness. They stay on the alert for signs of physical and/or emotional abuse, neglect and other family problems that might impair a student's school performance. If necessary, they will intervene and provide help or make appropriate referrals.

Although most of the problems and situations you'll encounter as a school counselor are rather mainstream, there is always the potential for a serious incident. For example, a student who sees you as a trusted adult might disclose that she is being sexually abused by her uncle. You must be prepared to deal with this scenario or anything else that might be thrown at you when you're working with youngsters.

Who Does a School Counselor Work With?

School counselors often work with students who have academic and social development problems, disabilities or other special needs. They also work with youngsters who aren't dealing with specific issues or those who don't have any particular disorder. Some students seek the general support and guidance that they don't receive at home. Others may need a neutral party to help them clarify an issue, or they may simply need to vent.

A school counselor's work can be done on both an individual and group basis. It may consist of individual sessions or group meetings with youngsters who have a particular disorder or are struggling with similar issues. She might also provide educational seminars for the student body at large on life skills or mental health-related topics.

School counselors typically act as advocates for students. They partner with other professionals and organizations to promote the academic, personal, social and

Although most of the problems and situations you'll encounter as a school counselor are rather mainstream, there is always the potential for a serious incident.

career development of the children and youths they serve. They often collaborate with teachers, administrators, social workers, psychologists, medical professionals and community service officers.

School counselors take a flexible approach that requires possession of a varied skill set. They use interviews, counseling sessions, interest and aptitude assessments, and other methods to evaluate and advise the students with whom they work. This helps them determine each youngster's individual abilities, interests, talents, and personality traits. School counselors use the information they collect to assist the students in developing realistic academic and career goals and tackling problem areas that might be impeding their performance.

At the high school and post-secondary levels, counselors may also run career information centers and conduct career education programs to help prepare older students for post-graduation work choices.

A typical client might be Seth, a high school senior who is undecided about what to do once he graduates. He's thinking about attending a community college to take computer-related classes, but he works part time at an auto mechanic shop and has been offered a full-time position after graduation. He enjoys working with computers, but he's also a talented mechanic so he needs help deciding on the right path. If he decides to go to college, he would need financial aid but isn't sure how to apply for it.

You would help Seth look at all his options objectively in terms of his personal preferences, aptitude, interest, and both short and long term effects on his life. Then you would guide him to the best decision for his situation.

Where Does a School Counselor Work?

School counselors can be found at every level of the educational system, from elementary school to postsecondary education, in both public and private institutions. They work in grade schools, junior high schools, high schools, colleges and universities. They are also employed by community colleges and technical, trade or vocational schools.

Some school counselors work strictly at one location, but others may travel between several different schools. If they are employed by a public school district or a college with satellite locations, they might spend designated days and hours at each location.

Additional Training for School Counselors

The Council for Accreditation of Counseling and Related Educational Programs (CACREP) outlines several requirements for degree programs in school counseling. Students who go through a CACREP-accredited program can be assured that their coursework and experience meet these standards.

Each state has its own licensure and/or certification requirements for school counselors. Often, licensure for this specialty is handled by a different board than the one that grants general mental health counseling licenses. For example, it may be administered by the state department of education rather than a health-related board. A link to the relevant state boards can be found on the American Counseling Association's website at www.counseling.org/PressRoom/NewsReleases.aspx?AGuid=78e3faf4-fbea-4ae3-a5ea-e44cd639ee3e.

School counselors may also choose to get national certification through the National Board for Professional Teaching Standards (NBPTS) or the National Board for Certified Counselors (NBCC). Each of these certifications has its own requirements for education, testing and experience, which can be found on their websites. NBPTS standards are listed at www.nbpts.org/the_standards and NBCC standards can be found at www.nbcc.org/certifications/ncsc/Default.aspx.

Some states allow a school counselor to use teaching experience in lieu of direct counseling experience as spelled out in their licensure requirements. Some licensing boards may specify additional classes that must be taken as a part of the degree requirement, such as dealing with gifted students or working with youngsters with special needs. If you are interested in becoming a school counselor, check out the specific requirements in the state where you intend to work.

How Much Does a School Counselor Earn?

A school counselor's salary can vary widely, depending on the place of employment. Those working at the elementary or secondary school level can expect to earn a mean annual salary of $57,830 as of 2007, based on figures from the Bureau of Labor Statistics. At a community college, a counselor can expect to earn a mean annual salary of $54,100, while the amount at colleges, universities and professional schools was $46,810 as of 2007. Besides being dependent on the workplace, salaries vary based on location and years of experience.

Professional Organizations for School Counselors

The American School Counselor Association (ASCA) supports counselors' efforts to assist students in focusing academic, personal, social and career development. By doing this, the ASCA strives to help students achieve success in school and be prepared to lead fulfilling lives as responsible members of society after they graduate. More information can be found on their website at www.schoolcounselor.org.

The American College Counseling Association (ACCA) is an organization for counselors who work in higher education setting, including colleges, universities, and community and technical college settings. It supports these professionals in their mission to foster students' development. Their website is www.collegecounseling.org.

The National Association for College Admission Counseling (NACAC) supports admission counseling professionals working at colleges and universities. The NACAC is committed to promoting high professional standards that foster ethical and social responsibility. More details can be found on their website at www.nacacnet.org.

This is just a sampling of school counseling-related professional organizations. You may be able to find others online, through your instructors in college, or through peer recommendations.

Sub-Categories

Because the specifics of a school counselor's job can vary so widely depending on the age group of the population served and the particular work setting, let's take a closer look at each sub-category into which a school counselor might fall:

Elementary School Counseling

School counselors at the elementary level work directly with students, but they also partner closely with teachers and parents to assess and evaluate youngsters. They determine whether further action is necessary and what interventions might be appropriate. Their work is especially important because early intervention can head off problems later in a child's school years.

Elementary school counselors determine an individual child's strengths and weaknesses in the areas of social and academic development and consider any other special needs or challenges. Based on this assessment, they can work with teachers and parents to create a customized plan that will help the child overcome barriers and reach his full potential.

Elementary school counselors also partner with teachers and administrators on curriculum development. They offer their expertise to help ensure that the curriculum will meet the academic and developmental needs of the student body.

Because they are working with younger children, elementary school counselors generally don't do vocational counseling, although they might touch on career choices in a very general way. Their academic counseling is limited to age appropriate goals and interventions. Academic counseling responsibilities are expanded for school counselors working at the middle school and junior high levels. Because they are dealing with older students, they help youngsters work towards academic success and prepare for the transition to high school. At this level, discussion of college and career options gets a bit more specific.

High School Counseling

When a student reaches high school, his decisions start to have far-reaching consequences because he's on the brink of a life transition. Choices such as whether to pursue a college education, study a trade or to enter the workforce immediately will affect his immediate and long-term future.

High school counselors assist students with day-to-day issues, but they also focus on the life choices faced by their charges as they draw closer to graduation. These professionals guide students in making sound choices that will prepare them for post-graduation life, whatever their direction might be.

High school counselors must be prepared to help all students, no matter what their future holds. They assist college-bound youngsters in navigating the maze of admission requirements, entrance exams, financial aid, and choosing a college and major. Because not every student is willing or able to attend college, they help others decide on trade or technical schools or coach them on job search skills that will prepare them for immediate entry into the workforce. This might include group or individual training in areas such as effective resume writing and how to prepare for a job interview.

High school counselors can help guide students into work/study partnerships and associations that help them gain on-the-job experience while still in school. These might include such organizations as the Business Professionals of America and the Distributive Education Clubs of America. They may also promote vocationally-based programs such as job shadowing, mentoring, community service projects, school-based business enterprises, internships, cooperative education, and apprenticeships.

College Counseling

Many colleges and universities have career planning and placement counselors. These professionals primarily work with students and recent graduates, although their services may also be available to alumni. They help clients with career development issues or assisting them in building job-hunting skills. These schools also employ admissions counselors who guide prospective students in making the best choices that pertain to their postsecondary education. College counselors may also provide support to special populations such as returning adults or students in remedial programs.

Post-secondary schools may also employee mental health counselors to provide general counseling and support to students. These professionals perform the same type of duties as mental health counselors in other environments. They address issues that are common to college students such as coping with stress, developing time management skills, dealing with social issues, honing study skills, goal setting, prioritizing, and maintaining motivation.

A typical client might be Louise, a freshman living on the college campus where you work. This is her first time away from home, and she misses her

50

family and friends. She's struggling with her coursework, even though her past records show that she's got good academic ability. You determine that the change in her life situation and loss of a local support system is behind her drop in grades. You help her develop new resources and show her how to refocus on her schoolwork so she can regain her former success and build on it.

Personal Insight

Sarah Maurer, a counselor at an international school, was inspired to enter this profession by her best friend. They met when they were both counselors at a summer camp, and she says, "We both really loved our jobs and connecting with the kids."

She's been doing it for several years now but says, "I still feel like I'm 'becoming'. School, while helpful, didn't prepare me for a lot of the job. Finding a good mentor is so important in those early years."

She finds that school personnel don't always understand what a school counselor does. "I often have to (gently) educate principals about my role," she explains. "Two of the three schools I worked at had weak counseling programs when I arrived."

Still, she loves her job because, as she says, "You essentially get to be the 'grown-up friend' to the kids at school. Can you think of anything better to do with your time?"

Is School Counseling the Right Career For You?

If this sounds like an area that might interest you, ask yourself the following questions. The more you answer with a "yes", the more likely it is that school counseling might be the right career choice:

- Would you like to work in an academic environment?
- Do you enjoy working with children and/or teenagers?
- Do you relate well to youngsters?
- Do you enjoy partnering with other professionals and work well as part of a team?
- Do you enjoy conducting interviews, tests and assessments?
- Do you like to work with groups as well as individuals?
- Do you enjoy conducting educational programs?
- Would you enjoy giving vocational guidance?

VOCATIONAL COUNSELORS
What Does a Vocational Counselor Do?

At its most basic, the role of a vocational counselor is to provide a positive link between clients who are seeking work and prospective employers who would be a good match. Some of their duties overlap with those of high school and college counselors, but their focus is strictly on career-related issues and skill building for job hunts. Rather than dealing with one specific population, they usually work with anyone who needs vocational guidance and assistance.

A vocational counselor typically helps clients by assessing their aptitude and abilities and helping them create realistic career goals based on the results. They also help people hone their job search skills and find appropriate prospective employers.

In some respects, a vocational counselor's job is similar to that of certain school counselors who work with older students. Some vocational counselors may even work in an academic setting, where they are often referred to as job placement counselors. There is also some overlap with rehabilitation counselors. Vocational counselors who help people with physical and mental disabilities to explore career options and find appropriate jobs often fall under the rehabilitation counseling umbrella.

Besides working directly with clients, vocational counselors have to maintain a high level of knowledge and awareness on current economic conditions and the job market. These continually changing factors might affect their clients' chances of success in their job searches.

Typical tasks performed by a vocational counselor include interviewing clients to gather information about their personality traits, educational background, work experience, skills, and interests. Often she will arrange or administer tests to measure achievement, aptitude, and occupational preferences. These efforts are aimed at helping clients to make the best career decisions.

Vocational counselors also work with individuals to develop job-search skills, locate prospective employers, and apply for appropriate positions. Additionally, they may provide support to people experiencing job loss, job stress, or other career transition issues.

At its most basic, the role of a vocational counselor is to provide a positive link between clients who are seeking work and prospective employers who would be a good match.

Who Does a Vocational Counselor Work With?

Vocational counselors work with people who are making their first foray into the workforce. They also assist clients who are currently working and need help in making career decisions, those who have been displaced by layoffs or job loss for other reasons, or people who are re-entering the workforce after a long absence.

In addition to providing direct services to these clients, a vocational counselor may also refer them to job training programs and organizations that can help them develop specific skills for entry or re-entry into the working world.

At the junior high and high school levels, vocational counselors often work with students, giving them guidance on selecting classes that will best prepare them for their eventual careers. They may also assist students in finding part-time jobs or summer employment and referring them to work/ school programs. For high schoolers who don't intend to go on to college, counselors can help them find a suitable job after graduation.

Depending on her client base, a vocational counselor might have a wide variance in the type of support she provides. For example, she might be working in a program to assist professionals who have been displaced from their long-time jobs by widespread layoffs. In this case, she would help them polish their resumes and brush up on interview skills. She would also help them locate prospective employers. If she's working at an agency that helps homeless people make the transition to entry-level jobs, her focus would be much more basic. She would help them find opportunities and prepare for interviews, but she might also assist with things like how to dress and appropriate social interactions in the working world.

Where Does a Vocational Counselor Work?

Many vocational counselors work for non-profit or government agencies that provide services for free. For example, they might work in a state employment office, a placement program for veterans, or a social service agency that receives government funding. In some offices, a vocational counselor will partner with an employment interviewer who does the preparatory work. The interviewer collects the initial information on the clients and passes it on to the counselor, who uses it to advise the client.

In a college placement office, the vocational counselor's role might be minimal. Clients are often fully trained and qualified. They simply need guidance in contacting prospective employers and preparing for the interview process.

In a social service agency, the vocational counselor generally takes a more comprehensive approach. Clients at these agencies are usually facing some sort of challenge. They may have had past difficulties holding onto a job for various reasons. These can run the gamut from a lack of training to a struggle with substance abuse or run-ins with the criminal justice system. Some may have run into prejudice due to their age, race, gender, religion or handicap. The counselor plays a supportive role in addition to providing concrete job search assistance.

Although vocational counselors typically work in an office, many spend time visiting job training centers and prospective employers. They interact with other professionals like instructors, company owners, and human resources personnel.

A typical client might be Mark, a 38-year-old male who worked for the same company for the past 10 years as a skilled laborer. Last month his employer closed its local manufacturing plant and terminated all of the employees. He received a severance package that included six months of pay and an extension of his medical benefits until the end of the year. He has a family to support, so he needs to get a new job before the severance funds run out. He's not sure whether he wants to stay in the same line of work or pursue something different.

Mark comes to a government office that provides assistance to displaced workers. He needs help assessing his interests and aptitude, a brush-up on his job search skills, and guidance on how to find appropriate opportunities.

You would assist Mark through the administration of tests to help him pinpoint appropriate fields. These would be based on the results, as well as an evaluation of his education and work background. You would help him prepare a new resume geared to these positions and refer him to an interview skills class, since he hasn't been on a job interview in a decade. Then you would help him locate potential jobs and offer support until he finds a new position.

Additional Training for Vocational Counselors

Generally there are no additional training requirements for vocational counselors over and above the usual requirements for a professional counselor. People who are interested in vocational counseling as their career might wish to take electives in interviewing and testing because these activities are commonly required on the job. They should choose as many electives as possible that are focused specifically on vocational counseling. If you know you are interested in this field, look for a master's program that offers a vocational counseling study track.

How Much Does a Vocational Counselor Earn?

Depending on their place of employment, a vocational counselor can expect to earn a mean annual salary between $36,070 and $57,830 as of 2007, based on figures from the Bureau of Labor Statistics. This can differ depending on where you work, your location, and years of experience.

Professional Organizations for Vocational Counselors

The National Employment Counseling Association (NECA) is a division of the National Counseling Association. It supports the professional development of professional counselors working in an employment or career development setting. The website is www.geocities.com/athens/acropolis/6491/neca.html.

There may be other professional organizations that support vocational counselors. You can search for them online or ask your instructors or colleagues in the field.

Is Vocational Counseling the Right Career for You?

If this field piques your interest, ask yourself the following questions. The more you answer with a "yes," the more likely it is that you would enjoy a career in vocational counseling:

- Do you enjoy guiding others through evaluations and decisions?
- Do you like to administer and interpret tests and assessments?
- Do you prefer to focus in one specific area of work?
- Do you prefer working with older teenagers and adults?
- Would you like getting out of the office to visit work and training sites?
- Do you enjoy staying abreast of the latest economic news?

REHABILITATION COUNSELING
What Does a Rehabilitation Counselor Do?

Rehabilitation counselors help people deal with the personal, social, and vocational effects of physical and mental disabilities. Their clients may be coping with challenges caused by a variety of circumstances, either life-long or recent. These include birth defects, illness, disease or the after-effects of an accident.

Rehabilitation counselors evaluate the strengths and limitations of the individuals they work with, provide personal and vocational counseling, and arrange for medical care, vocational training, and job placement. Their focus is on what a client can do rather than on the barriers and limits.

Who Does a Rehabilitation Counselor Work With?

Rehabilitation counselors work with people who are struggling with physical, mental or social disabilities. They interview these clients, as well as their family members, and evaluate school and medical reports. They also confer with a variety of professionals such as doctors, psychologists, occupational therapists, and employers to determine the capabilities and skills of the individual. Once they have enough information, they create a rehabilitation plan which may include training to help the client live independently and develop job skills.

Many rehabilitation counselors work with disabled youngsters in schools to coordinate rehabilitation and transition services. They also help disabled adults who are unable to hold full-time jobs by helping them find independent living services and supported/sheltered employment opportunities.

A typical client might be Yolanda, a 26-year-old woman who was badly injured in a car crash, resulting in permanent damage to her legs. She can walk with the aid of braces, but she can't stand for long periods of time. Previously she worked as salesperson in a furniture store, which entailed long hours of standing and walking. Her disability makes it impossible for her to return to that same line of work.

Yolanda has completed several months of physical therapy. Now she is ready to start exploring new employment options. She also needs general help in learning how to live with her condition.

Your work would focus on finding new job opportunities for Yolanda. You might help her enroll in a job training program for data entry, which would allow her to work while sitting down for most of the day. Because she can no longer easily manage the stairs in her apartment building, you'd also help her find more appropriate housing.

Increasingly, rehabilitation counselors are also providing help to older adults who are going through lifestyle changes and health problems. Many disabled workers are starting to take advantage of the rehabilitation counseling services through their employers, private rehabilitation companies, or employee assistance programs. While they may have been excluded from the workforce for a long time, they are seizing new opportunities that may allow them to re-enter it.

Where Does a Rehabilitation Counselor Work?

Rehabilitation counselors can be found in facilities dedicated to physical restoration, mental health, addictions and substance abuse treatment, and similar settings. They may also work for government agencies. In all of those environments, they provide direct hands-on services. Some also act as consultants to insurance companies, industrial and educational institutions rather than working directly with clients.

In addition to working in an office, many rehabilitation counselors spend time out in the field. They may be required to observe clients in a job environment, and they may also visit workplaces and talk to company owners or human resource personnel to develop employment opportunities.

Additional Training for Rehabilitation Counselors

In addition to any state licensure requirements, professional rehabilitation counselors may wish to pursue certification through the Commission on Rehabilitation Counselor Certification (CRCC). This organization is dedicated to promoting quality rehabilitation counseling services to clients with disabilities, and it also acts as an advocate for the rehabilitation counseling profession. Certification requirements can be found on the CRCC website at www.crccertification.com.

How Much Does a Rehabilitation Counselor Earn?

Depending on their place of employment, rehabilitation counselors were earning a mean annual salary between $29,460 and $44,460 as of 2007, based on figures from the Bureau of Labor Statistics. Potential wages vary, depending on workplace, location, certification/training, and level of experience.

Professional Organizations for Rehabilitation Counselors

There are several professional organizations for rehabilitation counselors. These include the National Rehabilitation Counseling Association (NRCA), which can be found online at http://nrca-net.org, and the American Rehabilitation Counseling Association (ARCA), which has a website at www.arcaweb.org. You may be able to find additional organizations online, through the instructors in your counseling program, or through recommendations from peers in the field.

Is Rehabilitation Counseling the Right Career for You?

If this specialty sounds intriguing, ask yourself the following questions. The more you answer with a "yes," the more likely it is that rehabilitation counseling might be the right career choice:

- Do you enjoy facing challenges in your work?
- Do you have a skill for motivating people?
- Would you enjoy working out in the field rather than staying in an office all day?
- Would you like the opportunity to do some consulting work?
- Would you like to have a wide range of choices for your potential workplace?

MENTAL HEALTH COUNSELORS
What Does a Mental Health Counselor Do?

Typically when a person pictures a counselor, they envision a mental health counselor or therapist in general practice. It's perhaps the most popular choice in the field because of the variety it provides. These counselors work with a broad spectrum of clients. They help individuals, couples, and families who are struggling with life issues or mental health problems.

Mental health counselors learn a variety of therapeutic strategies. They may favor one, or they may take an eclectic approach when they are working with clients. Their training qualifies them to deal with issues such as anger management, stress management, addictions and substance abuse, anxiety, grief, depression, low self-esteem, and even suicidal tendencies. As a mental health counselor, you'll help people with generalized issues like anxiety or depression and problems with a specific cause like job stress, marital problems, or parenting issues.

Mental health counselors often work closely with other mental health and medical professionals. If a client is on medication, they will be managed by a psychiatrist in addition to seeing a counselor for talk therapy. In this field, you may also work with psychiatric nurses, psychologists, social workers and school counselors, depending on your client's background and how he was referred to you for services.

Who Does a Mental Health Counselor Work With?

Mental health counselors might work with just about anyone, from children to adults to senior citizens. They often serve a diverse population in terms of age, race, background and culture that is strongly influenced by their choice of work environment. A mental health counselor in private or group practice might also choose to specialize in a particular population, such as children or teenagers, couples, or older adults. She might also focus on specific issues such as anger management, couples communication problems, or behavior disorders in children or teens.

A typical client might be Melody, a 46-year-old woman struggling with depression. She is the mother of three, and her last child recently left home to go to college. Her husband has a full-time job, but she's been a stay-at-home mom for the past 17 years and she's having trouble adjusting to the empty nest. She feels sad, lonely, and anxious and it's starting to affect her everyday life. She's having trouble falling asleep at night, she has crying bouts during the day, and she's beginning to isolate herself from friends.

Melody made an appointment at a counseling clinic when she realized that her symptoms were getting worse. She was taking an over-the-counter sleep aid almost every night and she was afraid to go to the store because she thought she might suddenly start crying right in the middle of an aisle. She wants to sort out her feelings, pinpoint what is causing her depression, and regain control over her life.

Your work would focus on the underlying causes for Melody's symptoms. It's likely that the major changes she's facing have triggered her feelings. Together you would create a plan aimed at helping her manage and process the feelings and regain control of her life.

Where Does a Mental Health Counselor Work?

Mental health counselors can work in a wide variety of environments, from private or group practice to government facilities to inpatient and outpatient clinics to social service agencies or employee assistance programs. They typically work in an office situation. Some mental health counselors provide in-home services, but it's not as common in this profession as it is in the social work field.

Additional Training for Mental Health Counselors

Mental health counselors generally don't require any additional training beyond a master's degree in counseling or a closely related field, particularly if the program is accredited by the Council for Accreditation of Counseling and Related Educational Programs (CACREP). CACREP accreditation offers some assurance that a program will meet most state licensing requirements for mental health counseling.

If you want to focus on a specific area in your practice, you can pursue additional learning opportunities. These include electives in your degree program, seminars, workshops, conferences, and continuing education classes. You can also read appropriate books and journals and join professional organizations focused on your interest.

How Much Does a Mental Health Counselor Earn?

Depending on their place of employment, mental health counselors were earning a mean annual salary between $31,550 and $59,590 in 2007, based on figures from the Bureau of Labor Statistics. Earning potential varies depending on workplace, location of practice, and experience level.

Professional Organizations for Mental Health Counselors

The American Mental Health Counselors Association (AMHCA) is a professional organization for members of the mental health counseling field. It seeks to enhance the mental health counseling profession through licensing, advocacy, education and professional development. Its website can be found at www.amhca.org. This is not the only organization that may be of interest to mental health counselors. You can find others online, through your college instructors, or via discussions with other professionals.

Is Mental Health Counseling the Right Career for You?

If you think this might be a field of interest, ask yourself the following questions. The more you answer with a "yes," the more likely you are to find fulfillment in a mental health counseling career:

- Do you like to work with a wide variety of clients and issues?
- Do you prefer a flexible work environment?
- Would you like the opportunity with work with groups as well as individuals?
- Would you like to have your own private practice?
- Would you like to choose your area of focus?

MARRIAGE AND FAMILY THERAPISTS
What Does a Marriage and Family Therapist Do?

Marriage and family therapists work with individuals, couples and families to resolve conflicts and develop healthy interaction skills. They focus on addressing family system issues, teaching communication skills and fostering respect among family members in order to resolve current problems and prevent or minimize future ones. They may also intervene in cases of family crisis and provide mediation in divorce and custody disputes.

Marriage and family therapists go beyond the traditional emphasis on the individual and work with people in the context of their primary relationship networks in marriage and the family system. Their approach is usually wide-ranging, and they focus on the long-term well-being of their clients.

Besides providing counseling sessions, marriage and family therapists often teach relationship and family skills classes on topics like parenting, communication, anger management and conflict resolution. Some target their work at specific areas, such as integrating step-families or helping divorcing couples develop their visitation plan.

Who Does a Marriage and Family Therapist Work With?

Because they're dealing with families as a whole, marriage and family therapists work with clients of all ages, from children up through adults. They might do individual, couples, or family counseling or various combinations as required by the situation. Sometimes they work with individual family members in separate sessions while also treating the entire family group.

A typical client might be the Miller family. Helen and Trent were married two years ago. He had a 10-year-old daughter and a 12-year-old son from a previous marriage, and now they have a year-old baby boy together. Although Trent's children like Helen, there have been some problems lately. The daughter, Tia, has been struggling in school, and her grades have slipped over the past year. The son, Jake, has been disrespectful to Helen and refuses to obey her when his father isn't around.

The Millers have come to a local counseling clinic that specializes in blended family issues. They are hoping to work together to resolve their problems and learn how to handle conflicts more effectively.

As a marriage and family therapist, you would help the Millers express their feelings to get to the root of the issues, For example, Tia disclose that she's feeling displaced by the new baby. Jake might say that he feels like Helen is trying to take his real mother's place. Further discussion might reveal that Trent is inadvertently reinforcing the problem by taking

Marriage and family therapists go beyond the traditional emphasis on the individual and work with people in the context of their primary relationship networks in marriage and the family system.

Jake's side in disputes. Once the family system problems have been pinpointed, you can help the Millers create a plan and work together to implement targeted solutions.

Where Does a Marriage and Family Therapist Work?

Most marriage and family therapists work in private practice, in group practice at counseling clinics, or at social service agencies. Many also work for government agencies that deal with family issues. They can be found in any work environment that focuses on building, supporting and maintaining the family unit.

Additional Training for Marriage and Family Therapists

Marriage and Family Therapists (MFTs) are mental health professionals with special training in psychotherapy and family systems. They are specifically trained to recognize and treat mental and emotional disorders within the context of marriage, couples and family systems. Almost every state currently issues a specific license for this profession. They designate "Licensed Marriage and Family Therapist" (LMFT) as a regulated professional title requiring the completion of specialized training.

How Much Does a Marriage and Family Therapist Earn?

Depending on their place of employment, a marriage and family therapist could expect to earn a mean annual salary between $39,410 and $60,490 as of 2007, based on figures from the Bureau of Labor Statistics. This varies depending on where she is employed, where she is located, and how much experience she has.

Professional Organizations for Marriage and Family Therapists

The American Association for Marriage and Family Therapy (AAMFT) is an organization that advances the professional interests of counselors working in this field. Their website is www.aamft.org. According to the AAMFT, there has been a 50-fold increase in the number of marriage and family therapists over the past 40 years. At any given point in time, they are treating over 1.8 million people in the United States.

There may be other organizations to support marriage and family therapists. You may find them online, through college instructors, or through your colleagues who may already be members.

Is Marriage and Family Therapy the Right Career for You?

If this sounds like an area in which you might like to practice, ask yourself the following questions. The more you answer with a "yes," the more likely it is that you would like a career in marriage and family therapy:

- Do you enjoy working with couples and families rather than just individuals?
- Are you interested in the ways in which members of a family system interact?
- Do you like to address communications issues?
- Do you like to guide people toward interacting more effectively?
- Would you like to have your own private practice?
- Would you like to focus on a specific area or issue that affects families?

SUBSTANCE ABUSE/ADDICTIONS COUNSELORS
What Does a Substance Abuse/Addictions Counselor Do?

As the name implies, substance abuse/addictions counselors help clients who are struggling with addiction issues. They may be abusing one or more substances such as alcohol or drugs, but addictions can take many other forms. A substance abuse/addictions counselor might treat people with eating disorders such as compulsive overeating, anorexia or bulimia. She might work with clients fighting other addictions, such as sex, gambling, spending excessive amounts of money, or internet pornography. The counselor's role is to help the client conquer his addiction and understand the underlying issues that caused and enabled it. She may refer the client to additional means of support, such as 12-step programs. Some substance abuse/addictions counselors also conduct addiction awareness and prevention programs in schools, at social service agencies, and in other forums.

Who Does a Substance Abuse/Addiction Counselor Work With?

Substance abuse counselors work with individual clients and/or conduct group therapy. They might also have opportunities to interact with a client's extended family. Some clients may seek out treatment on their own, while others may have been urged by family members through an intervention or by their supervisor or a co-worker through an employee assistance program. Some enter treatment because their addiction has landed them in legal jeopardy and they've been ordered to do so by a judge as a way to avoid jail time.

Clients may come to you for counseling on their own, or they may be referred for a continuation of treatment after being released from an inpatient program. If they've been hospitalized, you might work with other professionals such as psychiatrists or psychologists to coordinate treatment. You may also work with clients who are simultaneously attending a 12-step program or other recovery group.

A typical client is Ralph, a 40-year-old factory worker who has been struggling with a drinking problem for the past 12 years. At first it was limited to the weekends. He would stay sober Monday through Friday, then party all day Saturday and spend Sunday nursing a hangover before starting the cycle all over again. Lately he has started drinking during the week, too. At first he denied this, even though his wife found several bottles of vodka hidden in the garage. Then he was sent home from work and suspended for two days for being drunk on the job. His supervisor referred him to the company's Employee Assistance Program (EAP). After an initial assessment, he was referred to an outpatient treatment facility.

Your work with Ralph would focus on helping him achieve and maintain sobriety. You might refer him to a local Alcoholics Anonymous group so he has an additional support system. It may also be appropriate to hold a joint session with his wife so she can learn how to avoid enabling his negative and self-destructive behaviors.

Where Does a Substance Abuse/Addiction Counselor Work?

Substance abuse/addictions counselors are commonly found working at outpatient and inpatient treatment centers. They may also be employed by government agencies or social service agencies or run treatment programs in correctional facilities. Some substance abuse/addictions counselors prefer to run their own private practice.

Additional Training for Substance Abuse/Addiction Counselors

Substance abuse/addictions counselors generally get their master's degree in counseling or a closely related field, but they might take a concentration of elective courses focused on the theory and treatment of addictions issues. They may spend their practicum working in a substance abuse/addictions treatment setting to gain hands-on experience in the field.

Some states offer certification for substance abuse counselors. This is separate from a counseling license and represents compliance with classroom and experience requirements specifically in the area of substance abuse/addictions as designated by the certifying agency.

Certification is also offered by the National Board for Certified Counselors (NBCC) in conjunction with the American Counseling Association and International Association of Addiction and Offenders Counselors. Further information can be found on the NBCC website at www.nbcc.org/certifications/mac/Default.aspx.

How Much Does a Substance Abuse/Addiction Counselor Earn?

Depending on their place of employment, a substance abuse/addictions counselor was earning a mean annual salary between $33,380 and $42,430 in 2007, based on figures from the Bureau of Labor Statistics. The earnings potential for this field varies, depending on workplace, location, certification, and length of experience.

Professional Organizations for Substance Abuse/ Addiction Counselors

The National Association for Alcoholism and Drug Abuse Counselors (NAADAC) is an organization serving addiction counselors and other addiction-focused health care professionals. Its members specialize in addiction prevention, treatment, recovery support and education. (www.naadac.org.)

The International Association of Addiction and Offenders Counselors (IAAOC) is an organization for counselors who work in the addictions and forensic/criminal justice fields. Its website is www.iaaoc.org.

There may be other organizations geared towards substance abuse professionals. You might find them online, through instructors in your college program, or through the recommendations of your peers.

Is Substance Abuse/Addiction Counseling the Right Career for You?

If this sounds like a field that you might enjoy, ask yourself the following questions. The more you answer with a "yes," the more likely it is that substance abuse counseling might a good career option:

- Do you enjoy being part of a team?
- Do you like to work in a structured environment such as a hospital or treatment facility?
- Do you like focusing on one specific area of practice?
- Can you be both tough and supportive to clients?
- Would you enjoy doing both individual and group work?

OTHER TYPES OF PROFESSIONAL COUNSELING

There are other types of counseling that are less common than the categories discussed earlier in this chapter, but many of them are experiencing rapid growth because they've come into being in response to growing needs in society. Two examples, which are being driven by the changing demographics of American society and technological advances, are gerontological counseling and genetic counseling.

Gerontological Counseling

According to the Department of Health and Human Services Administration on Aging, in 2006 there were 37.3 million people age 65 and older in the United States. By 2030, the administration estimates that this number will grow to 71.5 million. As it skyrockets, the field of gerontological counseling has sprung up to meet the needs of this expanding group.

Gerontological counseling involves working with aging adults and their family members to help them ease their life transition. Counselors in this field might have a private practice or work for a government or social service agency, health care provider, or residential facility.

Genetic Counseling

As medical tests become more sophisticated, so does risk assessment and early diagnosis of diseases. Patients are able to find out whether they have a genetic predisposition to certain conditions and the likelihood of developing a particular disease. Expectant parents learn early on about potential genetic risks and birth defects in the children they are carrying. Genetic counselors specialize in working with these populations.

Some genetic counselors work with couples who want to have children but who have genetic risk factors or face other circumstances that increase the likelihood of a birth defect. They help potential parents make informed decisions on assumption of risk and family planning.

Another aspect of genetic counseling is working with adults who have discovered that they're at heightened risk for certain conditions or diseases. A genetic counselor helps them deal with the risk and shares information about the disease.

Although similar information may be widely available online or through books and other publications, counselors add a personal touch to the patient education process. In a study of women at moderate risk of breast cancer, researchers found that a majority favored talking to a genetic counselor versus having information delivered by a computer (Green, McInerney, Biesecker & Fost, 2001). Counselors can put clients at ease, exhibit sensitivity for their concerns, help them feel listened to, and guide them through tough decisions.

WORKING WITH SPECIFIC POPULATIONS AND ISSUES

Even if you choose to go into general mental health counseling, you may elect to provide services with a specific slant or focus on a particular population. For example, you might specialize in relationship work with gay or lesbian couples; family counseling for adopted youngsters; or supportive counseling for adolescents who are underachieving in school. You might specialize in brief therapy, which typically involves only one or two sessions, or advertise yourself as a Christian counselor who combines psychological theory with Biblical tenets.

Although you can't earn a targeted degree in most of these specialties, many schools offer individual classes that focus on working with specific populations. You can also choose a workplace for your practicum and internship where you will work with your population of choice or be allowed to focus on a specific type of therapy.

Often you will be able to find a professional organization that allows you to network with other counselors who share the same interests. For example, the Association of Lesbian, Gay, Bisexual & Transgender Issues in Counseling (ALGBTIC) supports counselors working with these populations. Those who meld traditional counseling with Biblical principles can find support in the American Association of Christian Counselors (AACC). The National Association of Adoption Counselors (NAAC) is a professional organization for those who help adopted children and their families make a smooth adjustment. The website addresses of these organizations can be found in the Resources section at the end of this book. These are just a few examples of the many areas of interest in which you might concentrate and find support among others with the same focus.

You may also want to specialize in clients who are focused on a particular issue. For example, you might choose to do grief counseling, helping people work through losses and the various stages of the mourning process. There are associations for counselors working with many specialties. For example, grief counselors can join the Association for Death Education and Counseling (ADEC) for support in working with clients dealing with the loss of loved ones. Their website is listed in the Resources section.

CHOOSING YOUR FOCUS

To choose the field that suits you best, ask yourself the following questions:

- What age group would I prefer to work with? Do I enjoy working with children, or would I rather serve a more mature client base? Are there particular life stage issues that I would like to focus on?
- What work setting would I prefer? Do I work best in a structured environment or would I prefer more freedom and autonomy? Would I like working outside of the office and interacting with a wide variety of people?
- Would I prefer to work with individuals, or would I enjoy group work too? The distinction between individual and group work can be an important one. According to New York psychologist Patricia Berlinger, group counseling involves a much different dynamic. "I do mainly one-on-one counseling because I have a hard time concentrating on more than one person at a time," she says. In group work, "you have to get the overriding themes of the group and are not able to stay with the fullness of each individual."
- Would I thrive on variety rather than the same set routine or dealing with the same issues repetitively? The author of this book has an in-person practice and also counsels clients online. She enjoys computer-based work because it allows her to help people with a wide variety of issues, from parenting and relationship problems to addictions and compulsions.
- What sort of issues would I prefer to help people sort out? Personal problems? Family conflicts? Education or career related questions? Managing emotions such as anger, stress, depression, and grief? Something else?

- Is there a particular group I would like to work with? Do I see a population that I feel is being under-served? Do I feel strongly about certain causes and issues? Could I support them through my work?

Personal Insight

Jason Fierstein, LPC, a licensed professional counselor in Arizona, works with men who are striving to improve their lives and relationships. He chose this population because, "I wanted to create a niche market for myself that I truly loved working with and where I felt was most effective. I have the most personal experience along my own journey as a man, and wanted to help other men who were struggling in their relationships."

He could see the need and demand for this niche. "I encountered men succeeding in all things worldly and material, yet when it came to relationship success, a lot of men didn't have a clue," he explains. "And the women--girlfriends and wives--were e-mailing and calling me to initiate counseling for their men. It was all making sense: I wanted to be the counselor that could more easily bridge that gap for these men, and help them to make their women happier, because they didn't know how to do this alone. They needed help.

"My own dad taught me a lot, but didn't give me all the tools that I needed to create real and lasting success in my relationships. I had to teach myself these things. I know that other men are in this position, and worse off, but don't seek the help out that they need. I wanted to help, saw the need, and am starting to speak to that need here in Phoenix. I want to teach others what I have learned on my journey through manhood and as a relationship partner."

Jason is very content with his niche. He says, "Specializing in working with men is very rewarding for me. I really enjoy being part of the change process with other men, and working with them to stay in their marriages, improve the quality of life for themselves and their wives or girlfriends, and finding peace of mind and happiness."

CHAPTER SUMMARY

- There are several common fields that a professional counselor might choose: school counseling, vocational counseling, rehabilitation counseling, mental health counseling, marriage and family therapy, and substance abuse/addictions counseling.
- There are some new but expanding fields, such as gerontological and genetic counseling.
- Some mental health counselors focus on working with a certain population or group or limit their practice to addressing a specific issue.

For example, they might choose to work exclusively with adolescents or with men or women, or they might specialize in treating clients with anger management issues or problems in their relationship.

- There are professional organizations for virtually any specialty or focus.
- Anyone who is interested in the professional counseling field should consider which specialty might be most suitable. This decision should be based on growth and earning potential, work conditions, the population served and the typical job duties of each specialty.

THERAPEUTIC SPECIALTIES

In addition to the various specialties in the counseling field, there are also a number of therapeutic specialties. These involve treating a specific issue such as sexual dysfunction or using a specialized intervention like art or music therapy to facilitate work with clients. Often these techniques are used with people who have difficulty expressing themselves through conventional means or children and others who don't have the verbal skills to share their thoughts and feelings in detail.

Therapeutic specialties are normally carried out by licensed counselors who undergo additional training and certification as spelled out by the relevant professional organizations and sometimes by state licensing boards. This chapter discusses several examples of common specialties you might wish to consider.

SEX THERAPISTS

Sex therapists do work that is similar to general mental health counseling, but rather than covering a wide range of issues, they focus on sex-related problems. These may include sexual addiction, low or decreased desire for intimate contact, desire discrepancies in couples, erection problems, premature ejaculation, aversion to sex, and painful intercourse. Some of these problems can have a physical basis, but clients who have been given a clean bill of health by their medical doctors may have a psychological issue. Sex therapy may be conducted individually, partners may attend the sessions together, or there may be a combination of individual and couples work.

Although both partners may attend sex therapy, their work will be somewhat different than traditional couples counseling. Instead of focusing on relationship dynamics, decision making, communication, and other areas that affect the partnership as a whole, sex therapy focuses specifically on the couple's sex life, the specific dysfunction they're facing, all of the areas it's affecting, and how it can be remedied.

Growth Potential

Sex was once a taboo subject that wasn't discussed outside of the bedroom. It's now becoming more acceptable to talk about sex in general and admit to having sexual problems. Ads for Viagra and similar drugs pop up regularly on TV, and this openness is spilling over into the field of therapy as people become more willing to get help for intimate issues. As this trend continues, the field of sex therapy will grow accordingly.

Earning Potential

Although earnings vary based on location and workplace, a sex therapist in private practice makes an average of $75 to $100 per hour. Therapists working for an employer usually make somewhat less. Certified sex therapists can expect to make more money than those with no formal qualifications in the field.

Training Requirements

Most sex therapists are licensed mental health professionals in counseling, marriage and family therapy, or psychology who have taken additional training to qualify them for this specialty. Some states spell out specific requirements for sex therapists, while others don't offer a license for this specialty. In these states, practitioners need to have a general counseling license.

Two organizations that offer certification for sex therapists are the American Association of Sex Educators, Counselors, and Therapists (AASECT) and the American Board of Sexology (ABS). The AASECT requires candidates for its sex therapist certification to have at least a master's degree in a mental health-related field and a certain level of professional experience, as well as additional training and supervised work specifically in the area of sex therapy. More information can be found on their website at www.aasect.org.

The ABS certifies sex therapists who meet specific degree and experience requirements and who have taken a set of core courses in the field of human sexuality. They must also earn supervised experience in the field of sex therapy and endorsements from diplomats of the board. Full requirements are listed on their website at http://americanboardofsexology.com.

Sex therapists who wish to provide counseling with a Christian slant can apply for certification from the American Board of Christian Sex Therapists (ABCST). Their requirements are similar to the AASECT and the ABS, but they also require training the theology of sexual issues. More information can be found on their website at www.sexualwholeness.com.

Is Sex Therapy the Right Career for You?

The following questions should help you determine whether sex therapy would be a good career choice:

- Do you have a talent for putting people at ease when they're tackling a tough subject?
- Are you are non-judgmental?
- Are you able to discuss sexual topics without embarrassment?
- Can you help clients relax and open up about intimate issues?

ART THERAPISTS

Art therapists use the creative process to help clients express themselves, explore their feelings, gain insights, work through emotional conflicts and work through various other issues. The medium used can be anything from drawing, painting or photography to sculpting or modeling with clay.

Although they may work on their own, art therapists frequently partner with other mental health and education professionals such as counselors, psychologists, social workers and teachers. They find ways to integrate art therapy into a particular client's treatment goals when appropriate.

Art therapy can be used for clients of all ages, from children up through older adults. Kids who are still too young to have well-developed verbal skills can often express themselves through artwork. Elderly clients can maintain and improve their muscle tone and motor skills through many types of art therapy, such as creating pottery and clay art. Any person of any age who has difficulty with verbal expression and sharing emotions through words may find it easier to communicate through art therapy.

Artwork can also be used as a diagnostic tool. For example, the House-Tree-Person assessment asks a person to draw those three objects. Then the therapist asks various questions such as, "How old is the person?" and "What type of tree is that?" The client's projective responses can yield valuable information. The Diagnostic Drawing Series also involves the creation of artwork. The client is directed to draw any picture, using colored chalk pastels on a specifically sized piece of paper. Next he is told to draw a tree, and finally he is asked to draw his feelings using shapes, lines and colors. The therapist draws information from the placement of objects on the paper, color use, and other factors.

Any person of any age who has difficulty with verbal expression and sharing emotions through words may find it easier to communicate through art therapy.

Growth Potential

Art therapy has tremendous growth potential because it is very effective with several growing populations. More youngsters are being diagnosed with autism, Aspergers, and similar disorders, and many of them struggle to express themselves verbally. Art therapy can be a useful tool to engage them and give them tools to express themselves. The population of older adults is growing, too, as Baby Boomers age. Art therapy gives them a way to gain physical benefits like improvement of muscle tone and motor skills while also expressing themselves and releasing their emotions through their artwork.

Earning Potential

According to the American Art Therapy Association (AATA), entry level art therapists can expect to earn an income of $32,000. For those with experience, the median income is $45,000 annually. Earning potential varies based on geographic location, employer, and the therapist's specific job duties. Art therapists in private practice, those who have a state license, and/ or those who have earned doctoral degrees can expect to earn up to $100 per hour. Certification will also boost your earnings.

Training Requirements

Art therapy typically requires a graduate degree. Master's programs in this field cover many of the topics that are found in a general counseling program, but they also include classes that are focused specifically on the theories and clinical use of art therapy.

The AATA offers approval to degree programs that meet its standards. You can find a list of colleges and universities that have received approval at www.arttherapy.org/educationschools.htm.

Art therapists who meet specific educational and experience requirements can apply for credentials from the Art Therapy Credentials Board (ATCB). Their requirements are listed on their website at www.atcb.org.

Is Art Therapy the Right Career for You?

The following questions should help you determine whether art therapy would be a good career choice:

- Do you enjoy and appreciate art?
- Do you enjoy experimenting with various techniques to draw out clients?
- Would you like incorporating art materials into your therapy sessions?
- Would you like to encourage creative means of expression rather than simply talking?

MUSIC THERAPISTS

Music therapists use music-based interventions to help clients address physical, cognitive, emotional and social needs and issues within a therapeutic relationship. Treatment methods may include listening to music, moving to it, singing, and even creating it. Clients who have difficulty expressing themselves through ordinary speech may find that they can do so through music. They often use it as a way of sharing and releasing their feelings. Many clients struggling with emotional issues become more motivated and engaged in their treatment when music is used. Rehabilitation patients benefit from the physical movement that music encourages.

Studies have also shown that music can have specific effects on various parts of the brain. For example, it has been proven to reduce depression and anxiety and increase social behavior in certain populations (Nayak, Wheeler, Shiflett, & Agostinelli, 2000). Therapists can use this information to integrate music into therapy sessions in a targeted manner based on the client's current mood.

Clients do not have to have any special knowledge or musical ability to benefit from this therapy. Its benefits are not tied into to any one activity or style of music. Once a qualified music therapist has assessed a client's particular situation, she can choose the most effective way to integrate music into the treatment plan.

Growth Potential

According to the American Music Therapy Association (AMTA), the future of music therapy looks bright because research continues to show its effectiveness for a variety of applications. The AMTA says that its benefits have already been proven in the areas of physical rehabilitation, Alzheimer's disease, and psychoneuroimmunology.

Earnings Potential

As of 2005, the AMTA reported that the average annual salary for music therapists working for an inpatient medical unit was $43,869. This will vary, based on the therapist's experience and area of specialization, as well as geographic location and certification status.

Training Requirements

Music therapy typically requires a graduate degree. Master's programs in this field cover many of the topics that are found in a general counseling program, but they also include classes that are focused specifically on the theories and clinical use of music therapy.

Studies have also shown that music can have specific effects on various parts of the brain.

73

The AMTA offers approval to educational programs that meet its standards. You can find a list of schools that have received approval at www.musictherapy.org/handbook/schools.html.

Music therapists who meet specific educational and experience requirements can apply for credentials from the Certification Board for Music Therapists (CBMT). Specifics can be found on their website at www.cbmt.org.

Is Music Therapy the Right Career for You?

The following questions should help you determine whether music therapy would be a good career choice:

- Do you have a love of music?
- Do you have an understanding of music theory and/or skills in its creation?
- Do you have a strong belief in the healing power of music?
- Do you believe that listening to music can have a profound effect?
- Do you believe that anyone can create some form of music?

DANCE THERAPISTS

Dance therapists use body movement to help clients who have difficulty expressing their emotions in a healthy manner. This therapy is based on the concept that movement and emotion are directly related, and it aims to strengthen the mind/body connection and improve both physical and mental well-being. It's suitable for just about anyone with the physical capability to make dance-like movements, but it's especially helpful for people who dislike traditional face-to-face therapy. Dance adds a component that goes beyond talking and into the realm of physical expression and energy release.

Growth Potential

Dance therapy dates back thousands of years. It was used by Native Americans and Aboriginal tribes, but it didn't gain popularity in modern society until the 1950s. A dance teacher named Marian Chace used dance to help psychiatric patients at a Washington D. C. hospital. Although these patients were usually unable to join group activities, they were responsive to Chace's therapy. Meanwhile, another dancer was volunteering in state hospitals across the United States. Through their combined efforts, dance therapy gained in popularity and the American Dance Therapy Association (ADTA) was formed in 1966. Over the past 50 years its popularity has continued to grow, making it a viable career option.

Dance adds a component that goes beyond talking and into the realm of physical expression and energy release.

74

Earning Potential

Dance therapists typically earn a salary comparable to that of other arts-based therapists. An average salary range would be $34,113 to $53,944, depending on location, experience, employer, and professional credentials.

Training Requirements

The ADTA issues Dance Therapist Registered (DTR) and Academy of Dance Therapists Registered (ADTR) credentials, depending on a person's professional qualifications. To qualify as a DTR, an applicant must have a master's degree in dance/movement therapy or a related field, plus specific training in dance/movement therapy curriculum. There is also a supervised internship requirement. ADTRs must meet additional experience requirements. Further information can be found on their website at www.adta.org.

Is Dance Therapy the Right Career for You?

The following questions should help you determine whether dance therapy would be a good career choice:

- Do you have a special interest in dance?
- Do you have any formal training in dance?
- Do you believe in the benefits of physical movement and energy release?
- Would you like to incorporate movement and rhythm into your counseling sessions?
- Do you believe that anyone can benefit from the healing power of dance?

DRAMA THERAPISTS

Drama therapists use drama and/or theater processes in their counseling sessions to help achieve therapeutic goals with their clients. This can take many forms, such as theater games, role playing, improvisation, puppetry, and even miming. Drama therapy is an active approach that helps participants tell their stories, express feelings, set goals, solve problems, and improve interpersonal relationship skills. It allows them to act out situations, try new behaviors, and take risks in a safe environment before incorporating them into everyday life. It's also a way of achieving catharsis for clients with emotional pain.

Growth Potential

Drama therapy is an expanding field in general, but it tends to go through growth spurts in times of war. When soldiers return home from combat, they often go through flashbacks related to post-traumatic stress disorder. Drama therapy helps them work through their feelings in a concrete, non-threatening way, relieving the pervasive thoughts, memories and nightmares.

Earning Potential

According to the employment website simplyhired.com, drama therapists can earn an annual salary between $37,000 and $52,000, depending on their location, experience, place of employment, and professional credentials.

Training Requirements

The National Association for Drama Therapy (NADT) offers a Registered Drama Therapist (RDT) credential. Applications are required to have a master's or doctorate degree in drama therapy from an NADT approved college/university or a degree in a related field such as drama/theater, counseling, psychology, or another type of art-related therapy. They must also meet certain experience requirements. Further information can be found online at www.nadt.org/rdtrequirements.htm.

Is Drama Therapy the Right Career for You?

The following questions should help you determine whether drama therapy would be a good career choice:

- Do you have any training or special knowledge in the area of drama?
- Do you like to use role plays and behavior modeling in your counseling sessions?
- Do you enjoy incorporating non-traditional strategies into your work?
- Do you like to use dramatic interpretation to encourage expression?
- Are you good at coaching and encouraging others?

POETRY THERAPISTS

Poetry therapy, sometimes known as bibliotherapy, is a way of using poetry and other forms of the language arts to assist with the therapeutic process. A poetry therapist may use any type of literature such as poems, stories, journal entries, fairy and folk tales and memoirs to guide a client in the healing process. Because many people relate to the characters or feelings in a story or poem, bibliotherapy can help them to get in touch with their inner emotions.

Poetry therapy is a very interactive process that may involve reading, writing, or a combination of the two. Poems and stories may be explored, interpreted and dissected to find themes relating to the client's own life and emotional journey.

Because many people relate to the characters or feelings in a story or poem, bibliotherapy can help them to get in touch with their inner emotions.

Growth Potential

Poetry therapy in its modern form has been around since at least 1925, when it was mentioned in a book as a way to treat emotional and psychological ills. It received more attention in the '60s, and as a result, the Association of Poetry Therapists was formed in 1969. This group morphed into the National Association of Poetry Therapists (NAPT) in 1981. Although poetry therapy is still not as widely known and utilized as other arts-based therapies, there were around 200 certified poetry therapists nationwide as of 2007. Because the number of poetry therapists is still relatively small, it's a field with healthy growth potential.

Earning Potential

The expected annual salary for a poetry therapist is similar to that of other art-related therapists. According to the Mississippi Hospital Association Health Careers Center, it can run from $30,700 to $43,200, with an average of about $36,600 annually. This varies based on employer, location, experience, and certification.

Training Requirements

Poetry therapists can apply for certification from the National Federation for Biblio/Poetry Therapy. Requirements include a state license in a mental health profession, and the applicant must go through additional training on using poetry therapeutically. She must also earn supervised experience. Details can be found on their website at www.nfbpt.com.

Is Poetry Therapy the Right Career for You?

The following questions should help you determine whether poetry therapy would be a good career choice for you:

- Do you enjoy literature?
- Do you have any type of literary background?
- Do you believe in the therapeutic benefits of reading, writing and interpretation?
- Do you believe that reading or writing poetry and other types of literature can help clients express themselves?

PLAY THERAPISTS

Play therapists use structured, play-based strategies in their counseling sessions. The play may be free-form, or the therapist might use dolls, accessories, board games and other tools. Although play therapy can be used with any client, it's especially appropriate for youngsters because, according to the Association for Play Therapy (APT), play is the language of children. This makes it particularly useful for working with kids from age three to about age twelve.

Play therapy helps children communicate, even if they don't have the verbal language to accurately express their feelings and thoughts, and gives the therapist insight into a child's inner thoughts and conflicts. It can also be used by the counselor to demonstrate and teach behaviors. Because play helps youngsters feel comfortable in therapy sessions, it can help to build and strengthen the therapeutic relationship. It also allows them to express thoughts and feelings that they might not be able to talk about directly, either because of fear or a lack of the necessary verbal skills.

Growth Potential

The field of play therapy has grown tremendously over the past 25 years. The APT started in 1982, and by 2006 it had almost 5,000 members. As more youngsters are diagnosed with autism, Aspergers, and other disorders that can impair communication, play therapy is likely to grow as a way to facilitate expression in those with verbal challenges.

Earning Potential

Although salaries for play therapists vary depending on experience, location, and workplace, the website Indeed.com reports an average annual salary of $50,000 and up in major urban areas. Professional credentials can have a positive influence on the therapist's earnings.

Training Requirements

The APT offers a Registered Play Therapist credential for licensed mental health professionals who meet additional training and experience requirements in play therapy. Specific information on these credentials can be found online at www.a4pt.org/ps.credentials.cfm.

Is Play Therapy the Right Career for You?

The following questions should help you determine whether play therapy would be a good career choice:

- Do you enjoy working with children?
- Are you willing to get down to a child's level to engage in play activities?
- Are you comfortable using play to build and strengthen the therapeutic relationship?
- Are you willing to use play as a means to help children express their thoughts and feelings?

Play therapy helps children communicate, even if they don't have the verbal language to accurately express their feelings and thoughts, and gives the therapist insight into a child's inner thoughts and conflicts.

CHAPTER SUMMARY

- Professional counselors may choose to specialize in a specific type of therapy or therapeutic method.
- Most of these specializations require a counselor to have a master's degree and be state licensed, as well as having additional training and experience related directly to the specialized therapy.
- Certifications or other credentials may be offered by professional organizations for these specializations.
- Sex therapy is one area of specialization that involves working with clients on issues related to a very specific area.
- Many therapeutic specializations are related to the arts. These include art, music, dance, drama and poetry therapy.
- Play therapy is a technique used primarily for working with youngsters between the ages of three and twelve. It uses play activities as part of the therapeutic process.

ONLINE COUNSELING

O nline counseling, also known as e-therapy, is a relatively new but rapidly expanding field within the area of professional counseling. As internet use becomes ubiquitous and more people become comfortable seeking and using online services, counseling is a natural extension. Instead of being limited by time and geography, a person in emotional crisis can link up with a qualified mental health professional literally within minutes.

WHAT DOES AN ONLINE COUNSELOR DO?

An online counselor's work activities are similar to those of an in-person mental health counselor or marriage and family therapist. However, her services are provided via a computer instead of in a physical office. Services may be synchronous, meaning that both parties are online and interacting with each other at the same time, or asynchronous, meaning that each person logs in at their convenience to take part in the discussion.

Synchronous sessions are most commonly conducted via an instant message system or text chat console. All communication takes place via typed text that goes back and forth in a real-time conversation. Virtual sessions may also be held via computer microphone or telephone and webcam, but these are less common because of bandwidth and equipment limitations. As technology continues to improve, they will most likely become more popular, blurring the line between online and face-to-face therapy.

Asynchronous sessions are conducted via email. The counselor and client exchange a series of written responses, prepared at each person's convenience. The counselor may also have the client complete written "homework" assignments for later discussion.

Counselors may limit themselves to synchronous or asynchronous services, or they may offer a combination. For example, a real-time chat session may be followed up with a written assignment that the client completes on his own time frame and sends to the counselor via email. The counselor may then return written comments, or they may hold another live chat session to discuss it.

Many traditional therapeutic techniques can also be used in a virtual environment, and studies are underway to measure their effectiveness when done online. There are already studies to back up the usefulness of cognitive e-therapy when used for several common problems presented by clients. Good results have been achieved with panic disorder (Carlbring, Ekselius & Andersson, 2003), depression (Christensen, Griffiths, & Korten, 2002; Christensen, Griffiths, & Jorm, 2004) and post-traumatic stress disorder (Lange, Rietdijk, & Hudcovicova, 2003).

Although e-therapy may seem impersonal and disconnected at first glance, research is showing that online counselors and their clients can establish a strong working alliance (Cook & Doyle, 2002). The counselor/client connection is necessary to conduct effective therapy sessions no matter what the medium.

Online counseling usually takes two forms: on-demand and ongoing. In its ongoing form, it's similar to in-person work. A client approaches the e-therapist for an assessment and arranges to enter into therapy. They have regularly scheduled sessions for weeks or months, depending on the complexity of the issue. When their work is done, they mutually agree to terminate it. For on-demand services, a person who is facing an immediate crisis or other emotional distress searches for an online counselor who is immediately available. He rings up the counselor and they conduct a brief therapy session focused on relieving the current stress. They may do work on an ongoing basis, but often it's just a one-time consultation.

For example, Maddie found a note in her husband's coat pocket that seemed to indicate he might be cheating on her. She confronted him and he admitted it and told her that he'd been unhappy in their marriage for the last two years. They had a big blow-out argument and he stormed out of the house. Maddie wasn't ready to share this with her family or friends, but she knew that she needed to talk to someone. She searched the internet and found an online counseling service with several professionals available for immediate sessions.

Based on descriptions of their expertise and qualifications, Maddie chose one of the e-therapists and connected for an instant messaging session. The therapist allowed her to vent and then helped her look at her options. They discussed what she would do when her husband returned home and what her long-term choices might be. They chatted for an hour, and by the end Maddie felt that she had calmed down and was ready to face the situation. She didn't want to schedule ongoing sessions; she just needed someone to talk to at that moment so she could work through her emotions and decide what to do.

WHO DOES AN ONLINE COUNSELOR WORK WITH?

Online counselors often work with a broader and more diverse client base than an in-person counselor. This is because online therapy is accessible to anyone, anywhere in the world, as long as they have an internet connection. Clients in some countries may have difficulty finding a local mental health professional, or they may be concerned about privacy, so they turn to e-therapists to get immediate, confidential help.

The privacy and depersonalized setting of online counseling often attracts clients who are dealing with particularly sensitive issues. Research has shown that these clients value the disinhibiting effects of conducting the session online (Cook & Doyle, 2002). People who seek online therapy due to the anonymity include married people who are having an affair; gay or lesbian clients who are not "out"; men dealing with impotence or other sexual issues about which they feel embarrassed; and clients with fetishes such as cross-dressing that they keep hidden in their everyday lives.

Online counselors stick to the same areas of competence that they would in face-to-face sessions. They screen clients to ensure that they have the appropriate expertise to handle the presenting the issue. This usually consists of having the client describe his issue briefly. If it fits within the counselor's scope of practice, she responds with a brief description of how she would approach it and information about informed consent. The client can then decide whether or not to engage her services. If it's outside her scope, she lets the client know and gives an appropriate referral if possible.

WHERE DOES AN ONLINE COUNSELOR WORK?

Some online counselors have a private practice and serve clients via their own individual website. They may offer e-therapy exclusively or as an adjunct to their in-person work. This means they are responsible for doing their own advertising and promotion to draw potential clients to their site. They must also have a means to provide the service and handle the billing. Many use an online payment processing service such as PayPal, which allows clients to use their bank account or credit card.

The privacy and depersonalized setting of online counseling often attracts clients who are dealing with particularly sensitive issues.

The majority of professional counselors working online do so as independent contractors for a service such as LivePerson. Their counseling section can be found at www.liveperson.com/experts/professional-counseling. These services provide virtual offices with chat and email capabilities, advertising, client referrals, and billing. In order to maintain the integrity of the service, they usually verify a counselor's license and other credentials before allowing her to join. As independent contractors, the participating counselors set their own hours and usually determine their own fees. For its services, the host site receives a percentage of each professional's earnings. Some host sites also charge a monthly or yearly fee in addition to the commission.

An online counselor must have the necessary space and equipment to support a web-based practice. At its most basic, this includes a reliable computer with a high-speed internet connection, an email account, and the means to conduct sessions through a secure instant messaging service. To maintain client confidentiality, the computer should be used exclusively by the counselor and should be password protected. It should also have up-to-date virus and spyware protection.

Counselors who use a visual and audio hook-up must have a webcam and PC microphone or telephone connection in addition to high speed internet. They must also have a dedicated office or other professional-looking workspace, since the client will be able to see and hear them just as they would in a face-to-face meeting. It would be very disconcerting for a person seeking professional services to see children burst into the room, to have a St. Bernard suddenly jump into the picture, or to see and hear soap operas blaring in the background.

At a minimum, online counseling requires:
- A computer with an internet connection
- A private workspace

Everything else is dependent on the type of e-therapy services you'll be offering and the forum you'll be using to do so.

GROWTH POTENTIAL FOR ONLINE COUNSELING

By 2010 it is estimated that over 90 percent of Americans will have internet access. According to the Institute of Medicine, up to 100 million Americans seek information about health online, including mental health issues. Counselors who enter the online field, either exclusively or as a complement to their in-person work, can tap into this continually growing market.

HOW MUCH DOES AN ONLINE COUNSELOR EARN?

Because most online counselors work in private practice or as independent contractors through other services, they set their own rates. This gives them control over their earnings based on their designated fees. Most earn a wage roughly comparable to a counselor in private practice or someone working in a group practice.

Those who provide their services through a commercial website can usually designate a per-minute or per-hour fee. They will pay a commission to the site for each session, and they may also be required to pay a monthly or yearly participation fee. Their rate must be high enough to offset these expenses and allow them to earn a profit. When working on a site with other counselors from whom prospective clients can select, they must keep their rate competitive so they don't price themselves out of business.

Online counselors who handle their own billing rather than working through a third-party site are responsible for clearly disclosing all fees, acceptable methods of payment, and collection policies to the client just as they would in a private in-person practice.

ADDITIONAL TRAINING FOR ONLINE COUNSELORS

Various classes and seminars in online counseling techniques are cropping up as the popularity of this medium continues to rise. Many of this training is stand-alone, but online counselors can earn a Distance Credentialed Counselor (DCC) credential through a program offered by the Center for Credentialing and Education, Inc., an affiliate of the National Board for Certified Counselors.

ONLINE COUNSELING SPECIALTIES

Just as an in-person counselor might specialize in working with specific issues or populations, e-therapists can focus on a certain niche. While there are inherent challenges in doing family and group work online, many other specialties can work nicely in the online realm.

Some e-therapists focus on common issues such as anger management, stress management, anxiety, or depression. Others take advantage of the privacy and depersonalized nature of online work to help people with potentially embarrassing issues. Online counseling encourages these people to seek assistance because they can do so in a "safe," confidential environment.

Specialties to help nervous/reluctant clients may include:

- Working with gay and lesbian clients, particularly those who are questioning their sexuality or who have not publicly "come out" yet.
- Working with transgender clients.
- Working with sensitive relationship issues such as infidelity that a client has not shared with his or her partner.
- Working with clients who are seeking help for potentially embarrassing issues such as internet porn or sex addictions.
- Working with clients who are struggling with fetishes such as cross-

dressing that they wish to keep private.

- Working with men who are coping with sensitive problems such as impotence or premature ejaculation.

As with any other form of counseling, you should only provide services in areas for which you are properly qualified.

BENEFITS FOR COUNSELORS AND CLIENTS

One of the reasons for the continued growth of online counseling is that it offers benefits to mental health professionals as well as to clients.

Counselor benefits include:

- *A flexible schedule.* Because they are working at home, online counselors can pick their hours. This allows a counselor juggling other household and family responsibilities to gear her schedule around them. Even e-therapists who work in the middle of the night can build a strong client base because they will get clients from other countries where the time difference makes it daytime.
- *Low overhead.* Although many online counselors also run an in-person practice, some conduct all of their sessions online. This eliminates the need to rent and furnish office space.
- *A built-in client base.* Online counselors who work as contractors through an established website don't have to do their own promotion. These websites typically have their own ad campaigns which drive traffic to the professionals who use them. Many online counselors promote themselves too through ads, links, and other means, but it's not absolutely necessary to run a successful online practice.
- *The ability to draw clients from a wide geographical area.* When a counselor practices exclusively via in-person sessions, her client base is limited to people within the immediate area. If she offers online counseling, her base of potential clients is virtually limitless. She may draw clients from throughout the United States and around the world.

Benefits for clients include:

- On-demand availability. Online counseling services allow clients to contact a qualified professional at any time of day or night for an on-demand session. Counselors can be found working around the clock seven days a week, including holidays. This provides an "emotional emergency room" for clients who are in acute mental pain and need immediate assistance.

Personal Insight

FROM THE AUTHOR: One New Years Eve, I brought my laptop computer to a party because I had a client who was going through a crisis. I wanted to be available for that person even though it was a holiday. Fortunately the client didn't need to contact me that night, but right at the stroke of midnight I was contacted by someone else. This new client had found my virtual office and noticed that I was available, so she initiated a text chat. While the other partygoers were dancing around with hats and noise makers, I was able to assist someone with an immediate emotional need. To me, this really underscored the power and immediacy of e-therapy.

- *Access to a mental health professional regardless of geographic location.* Some clients live in rural areas where therapists are hard to find. Others may be uncomfortable going to see someone in person because they live in a small, gossipy community where everyone knows everyone else's business. Online counseling gives every internet user access to a variety of professionals across the country.

- *Flexibility of session times.* Online counselors tend to have flexible schedules and offer their services at a wide variety of times, including evenings and weekends. Many potential clients are juggling work and family or have busy schedules for other reasons. In the online environment they can link up with a counselor who will work around their schedule.

- *In-home services.* Clients who are disabled, dealing with chronic illness, or homebound for any other reason can access a qualified counselor right from their keyboard. Online counseling can aid clients suffering from a fear if leaving their home, anxiety, or other issues that might make it difficult for them to go to an office. It also works well for those who simply prefer having a session in the comfort and privacy of their own home.

- *Access to affordable care.* Some counselors work exclusively online. They don't have to maintain an office, so their overhead is considerably lower than someone with a private in-person practice. This difference is often reflected in lower fees. A cheaper rate is particularly important for clients who might not have insurance coverage for mental health services and will be forced to pay out of pocket. It can also be a good choice for clients who have insurance but who prefer to pay directly in order to maintain their anonymity.

- *Being able to maintain privacy/anonymity.* Some services that provide virtual offices and handle the billing aspect will keep the client's personal information confidential and not automatically pass it on to the counselor. It can only be accessed in case of an emergency such as a suicide threat. This policy can build the comfort level of clients dealing with sensitive issues such as sexuality or infidelity because they know that their identity is protected.

• ***The ability to do a quick check in for specific issues rather than committing to ongoing counseling sessions.*** Online counseling is often a version of brief therapy in which clients only go through one or two sessions. If the problem isn't deep or serious, a one-time consultation can give someone enough information to resolve the issue as long as they're willing to apply the tools on their own.

Personal Insight

FROM THE AUTHOR: I've worked as an online counselor for several years, and I view it as sort of an emotional emergency room. When a person is in physical pain, they head for a hospital or urgent care center. When they're hurting emotionally, a counselor is as close as their keyboard.

I have a talent for talking people through a crisis and helping them make it through the emotion to see a glimmer of hope. That's why working online is especially fulfilling for me. When someone who was in the midst of turmoil when she contacted me ends the session by saying, "Thank you so much. I really feel better now," I know that I made the right choice when I decided to expand into e-therapy.

SPECIAL CHALLENGES FOR ONLINE COUNSELORS

If you're seriously considering becoming an online counselor, you should be aware of the special challenges you'll face and prepare yourself to work through them. Ask yourself the following questions:

• Am I confident that I can build a strong therapeutic relationship with online clients?
• Am I prepared to deal with the ethical issues involved in online counseling?
• Am I willing to keep abreast of the evolving developments and best practices in the online counseling field and to incorporate them into my practice?
• Am I aware of potential legal issues that may affect online counseling?
• Am I willing to use, maintain and upgrade the necessary technology to be an effective online counselor?
• There are several concerns that are present in face-to-face counseling but that require special care and consideration when working in the online forum. These include:
• Informed consent. An online counselor must inform the client about the therapy process, potential risks and benefits, safeguards, and alternatives. This should include special attention to the benefits of working with a

counselor face-to-face or finding local self-help groups vs. working online. The client should also be informed about the special risks to confidentiality that exist in the online world. These include the possibility of sending email messages to the wrong address or having someone access the session records on the client's or counselor's computer via password theft or because a shared computer is being used. The client should understand all of the risks and be aware of the alternatives before giving consent to services.

- **Protection against misunderstandings.** When counseling sessions are held online via instant messaging or email, misunderstanding can crop up more frequently than they would in an in-person session. The absence of voice inflection and non-verbal cues contributes to this risk. The counselor should warn clients of this potential and invite them to ask for clarification if they feel uncomfortable or misunderstood at any time.
- **Timely services.** Just as in-person counselors set up specific appointment times, e-therapists conduct scheduled sessions too. They should give these sessions the same priority that they give in-person work, since the computer is simply a virtual office and the work is basically the same. Online counselors who work with clients via email should let them know when they can expect a response and stick judiciously to that timeframe. They must be respect it with the same care that any other professional responsibility would be given. Because computers can crash, e-therapists should always have a back-up plan so they don't suddenly "abandon" a client due to technical challenges.
- **Identifying information.** Although the online environment lends itself to anonymity, a client should know the counselor's full name, contact information, and license/certification details just as he would if he were participating in in-person counseling sessions. If the counselor has additional training or other qualifications, this should also be shared with the client in detail.
- **Emergency plans and procedures.** If an online counselor isn't available in an emergency, there should be a back-up plan that provides the client with the name and number of a local mental health professional or doctor. Clients who are potentially suicidal should also have a contract in place, including an emergency plan, contact information for their local crisis line, and a verbal and written commitment to use it.

PROFESSIONAL ORGANIZATIONS FOR ONLINE COUNSELORS

The International Society for Mental Health Online (ISMHO) is made up of counselors who practice online and other professionals and students with an interest in online mental health services. It promotes the development and use of online communication tools, information and technology by the international mental health community, including counselors. Its website is www.ismho.org. As the popularity of e-therapy increases, other organizations may be formed. You will be able to find them online or through recommendations from colleagues.

IS ONLINE THERAPY THE RIGHT CAREER FOR YOU?

Online counseling may be the right career for you, either on its own or in tandem with a traditional practice, if you answer "yes" to most of these questions:

- Do you enjoy working with a diverse clientèle?
- Would you like to supplement a traditional counseling job with part-time flexible work?
- Do you need to be able to fit your work around a busy personal schedule?
- Do you have a physical challenge that makes it difficult to commute and work in a traditional office environment?
- Are you a fast typist?
- Are you comfortable with computers and online communication?
- Are you comfortable dealing with people who are going through an emotional crisis?

 *Personal Insight*

FROM THE AUTHOR: As an online counselor, one of the most enjoyable aspects for me is working with such a culturally diverse group of clients. I've counseled people in countries such as Canada, England, Australia, India and Africa. It has helped me develop a much greater empathy and appreciation for other cultures. It's still a bit amusing to be sitting at my laptop at midnight and have someone ring me up from the other side of the globe and greet me with a cheery "Good afternoon!" or to know that they're watching snowflakes outside their window while I sweat in the summer heat. The internet has truly made it a small world.

ISSUES RELATED TO ONLINE COUNSELING

Because online counseling is still in its infancy, there are many questions that need to be resolved. In the meantime, there are several gray areas that professionals must take into consideration before deciding to use this medium.

Legal Issues

At present there is no nationally recognized counseling license. Individual states handle their own licensing, which covers professional counselors working within that state. There is an unspoken assumption that clients will be coming to an office and receiving the services in the same location. Because of this, licensing requirements for online counselors are still murky.

An online counselor should be licensed in his state of practice, but the laws are currently unclear about whether this is enough to allow him to treat clients in other states. Some locales have laws that are aimed at curbing online medical diagnosis and prescription drug sales, and these could be interpreted to forbid intrastate counseling as well. The fact that e-therapy often crosses international borders adds another unresolved layer.

It could be assumed that when a client consults an online counselor, he is "stepping into" that counselor's virtual office in another state and receiving treatment in that jurisdiction. However, there is no legal precedent to back this up.

The American Association of State Counseling Boards (AASCB) is currently working to create a portability program for professional counseling licenses. You can read more about the AASBC in the chapter on licensure. This portability is aimed at assisting counselors who move from one state to another, but as online counseling becomes more common a similar reciprocity may someday be put into place for services provided at the keyboard.

In the meantime, if you plan to practice online counseling, check with professional organizations and your state licensing board for guidance. As e-therapy grows in popularity, the regulations will continue to evolve so they will be able to provide you will the most up-to-date information.

Threats to Confidentiality

Even though a counselor may abide by strong restrictions aimed at protecting the privacy of online clients, the client himself might inadvertently compromise his own confidentiality. This can happen if there is spyware on his computer or if someone in his household manages to find his password. These things are out of the counselor's control; all she can do is warn clients and leave the choice to them on whether they believe the benefits outweigh the risks.

Liability

Because of the newness of online counseling, it is not covered by some professional liability policies. Before you decide to offer e-therapy, check with your insurance company to make sure that you'll be covered in case of a legal claim.

STANDARDS AND ETHICS

While state boards typically require licensed counselors to abide by a code of ethics, most of these codes were written before online counseling started to enter

An online counselor should be licensed in his state of practice, but the laws are currently unclear about whether this is enough to allow him to treat clients in other states.

the mainstream. Thus they don't specifically address the points that are exclusive to e-therapy. Some professional organizations are stepping into the void to offer specific guidance on the provision of online counseling services.

The National Board of Certified Counselors has identified standards for the practice of web counseling. This information can be found on the NBCC website at www.nbcc.org/AssetManagerFiles/ethics/internetCounseling.pdf. If you're considering becoming an internet counselor, these standards contain some critically important points to consider, both ethically and logistically.

The American Counseling Association also addresses online counseling in their overall Code of Ethics. More information can be found at www.counseling.org/Resources/CodeOfEthics/TP/Home/CT2.aspx.

POPULATIONS THAT REQUIRE CAUTION

While online counseling can be used successfully with many different populations struggling with a variety of issues, there are certain people for whom it may not be suitable. Others may be able to benefit, but only with special precautions. As an e-therapist, you must be prepared to screen prospective clients to see if they fall into either of these groups. For the former, you should explain why online work is not advisable and refer them to more appropriate in-person help. For the latter, make sure that you put the appropriate precautions into place before you conduct any counseling sessions.

Take caution with any of the following clients:

- ***Children under age 18.*** Instant messaging is second nature to many adolescents and teens, so e-therapy may work well for them. This might not be true for younger children who don't have the capability to communicate effectively and build a strong therapeutic relationship online. If you're approached to provide services for a minor, be sure to do a careful screening before you agree to do so. When you're doing traditional therapy, it's easy to get parental consent that allows you to provide treatment to a youngster. The parents can read the forms in your office, ask any questions, and sign them in your presence. In the online environment, it's more difficult to get this permission and confirm that it's being provided by the parent because a teenager can easily forge a signature. Confirm the signer's identity by requiring his signature to be notarized. You can also request a copy of a driver's license or other official form of identification.

- ***Suicidal clients.*** Dealing with suicidal clients is a challenge in any forum, but online counselors face a particularly task when working with this population. When you can't observe someone's body language or hear the inflections in his voice, it's hard to asses his risk of self-harm. While you can administer a self-report assessment, the results are only accurate if the client responds to the questions honestly. Because of the anonymity of the internet, it may be difficult to summon help if he sends a suicide threat or decides to make an attempt during a session. Because of these limitations, many online counselors screen potential clients who present with depressive symptoms very carefully for suicidal tendencies. If they exhibit a likelihood of engaging in self-harm, they are referred to an in-person therapist or a local crisis line if they appear to be in imminent danger.

- **Potentially violent clients.** People who may pose a danger to others often fall under mandated reporting requirements. This can be complicated by the anonymity of internet work. Clients seeking treatment for anger management or related issues should be screened carefully. If there is a history of violent behavior or other red flags, the person should be referred for face-to-face work.

- **Clients who are not computer literate.** Even though the majority of American households have an internet connection, there are still people who have difficulty using a computer. They may stumble across an e-therapy website, but their skills might not be strong enough to use online counseling effectively. During the initial stages of your work, look for signs of difficulty that might indicate a lack of computer literacy. Is the client having trouble using the instant messaging service or attaching files if you're doing email therapy? If you notice these problems and they're impairing the effectiveness of your sessions, you may need to refer the client to an in-person counselor.

SUPPORT FOR ONLINE COUNSELORS

While all counselors benefit from professional support and networking, it's particularly important for those who practice online. Because of the newness of this field, it may be a bit of a challenge to find resources geared specifically to online counselors. Fortunately, as this specialty grows, the support options are expanding too.

The ISMHO has an online discussion group that allows professionals to network, share information, and discuss issues that are relevant to e-therapy. Some websites that provide virtual offices for online counselors also provide support services such as newsletters and private discussion forums. You can even find supervisors who specialize in providing supervision for e-therapists. Typically they work from virtual offices of their own and conduct their sessions online. This is valuable not only for the expert guidance and support but also for giving online counselors a taste of what it feels like to be on the other side.

Journal articles are also a good source for the latest research and news on e-therapy. They can be found online or in college libraries.

Personal Insight

Kathleen Finnegan, LPC, an online counselor working via LivePerson, says that she "fell into online counseling. I discovered it while looking for places to advertise my practice and found it immediately gratifying. I am a humanist and empath, as well as a fast typist, and find the act of using my hands, heart and head quite effective."

She says, "I keep a strong intent to do no harm, and when someone says 'I feel better now, thanks.' I feel the gift of happiness...and sometimes joy."

While she used to feel challenged by not seeing the client's emotional reactions, she explains, "Now I just ask the question: 'how are you feeling now?' and/or go with my intuition."

CHAPTER SUMMARY

- Online counseling is a growing profession within the counseling field.
- Online therapy is conducted on a computer using synchronous chat via an instant messaging service or asynchronously via email. Less commonly, a webcam and audio connection may be used.
- Online counselors often work with a very diverse population since e-therapy is available to anyone with an internet connection anywhere in the world.
- Online counseling has many advantages for both counselors and clients, such as ease of access and flexibility, but there are also drawbacks such as an inability to guarantee confidentiality and questionable legality of practicing across state and international borders.
- Online therapists should take care when dealing with certain populations, such as minors, suicidal clients, potentially violent clients, or those whose computer skills might not be strong enough to use online counseling effectively.
- Professional organizations such as the National Board for Certified Counselors (NBCC) and the American Counseling Association (ACA) have standards for online practice.
- E-therapists can find support from organizations such as the International Society for Mental Health Online (ISMHO), from supervisors with expertise in online counseling, and through articles in professional journals.

SALARY AND LONG-TERM OUTLOOK FOR PROFESSIONAL COUNSELORS

Counselors fulfill a vitally important role in society. They help people regain control of their lives, change ineffective behaviors, and deal with disorders and issues in a healthy, productive ways. Unfortunately the typical compensation isn't quite in line with the job's importance and responsibility level. Unless you manage to land your own talk show and gain celebrity status, you're not too likely to get rich working as a mental health professional.

TYPICAL SALARIES

Even though you're probably not going to become a millionaire or hit the jackpot as the next Dr. Drew or Dr. Phil, you can still expect to make a decent living wage as a professional counselor. Although the numbers change every year, in 2006 counselors were earning an average of $47,530 according to U. S. Department of Labor Bureau of Labor Statistics (BLS).

This figure can vary widely among specialties. The highest paid professionals were school counselors working at the elementary and secondary school levels, earning an average of $53,750 per year. Counselors providing vocational rehabilitation services were at the low end of the pay scale, earning an average of $31,340 per year. That's over $20,000 less than their school-based counterparts.

There are three factors that can have a significant impact on your earning potential as a professional counselor: years of work experience, employer/ workplace, and the state in which you are practicing. You can't control years of experience; that's something you have to earn over the course of your career. Fortunately you have immediate control over the other two factors. When you earn your degree, you can choose the state in which you plan to practice and obtain your license there. Once you've completed the licensure process, you can focus your job search on certain types of employers that tend to have a higher pay scale.

PRIVATE PRACTICE

Self-employed counselors who have managed to build up a solid client base typically earn the highest salaries. Because they are essentially running their own business, they reap all of the financial awards. They have job security because they cannot be fired. As long as they can attract clients, their job is secure.

This income level doesn't come easily because working on your own has its own set of challenges. You're responsible for the start-up costs and the ongoing overhead and expenses of maintaining an office, including rent, furniture, and utilities. You'll also have to pay for professional liability insurance. You'll shell out money for advertising and promotion as you work to build up your practice.

When you work for yourself, you won't receive the paid benefits offered by traditional employers, such as medical insurance and paid vacation time. You'll have to foot the bill for your own insurance, and when you take time off you'll lose income during that period and may also lose potential business from new clients.

Although technically you can set your own hours, in the early days of your practice you may find yourself scrambling. You'll be forced to work overtime to meet the start-up costs and get yourself established.

GROUP PRACTICE

Counselors who work in group practices are also near the top of the earnings scale, although below school and government jobs. If you join a group practice, you'll do the same type of work that you would in a private practice, but you won't shoulder all of the expenses. This makes it an attractive option for many mental health professionals who want to work in a private environment rather than an agency but who don't want to take on all of the responsibilities and risks.

There are three factors that can have a significant impact on your earning potential as a professional counselor: years of work experience, employer/workplace, and the state in which you are practicing

Employee or Independent Contractor?

When you're working in a group practice, you will either be considered an employee of the group or an independent contractor. Knowing the difference is critical because if you don't, you could be holding the bag for a significant tax burden at the end of the year.

96

Independent Contractors

If you're an independent contractor you won't have a supervisor in the traditional sense of the word. There won't be someone who acts as your boss, although you may have a supervisor for guidance and mentoring. If you're still in the licensure process, this will also be the person who documents your hours and fills out any paperwork required by the licensing board. However, she won't dictate the specifics of your work practices.

Because you're technically self employed, you'll have full control over your work schedule, the clients you choose, and the way you run your practice within the established rules of the group. You'll also be fully responsible for Social Security and Medicare taxes as well as the usual state and federal income taxes. Most likely you will be required to pay quarterly installments, and you'll receive a 1099 form listing your income at the end of the year rather than the W4 form given to employees.

Independent contractors do not receive any benefits and are responsible for their own medical and professional liability insurance, just like counselors in private practice. The main benefit lies in sharing facilities and expenses with others in the group and reaping the potential rewards of a higher income.

Employees

If you're an employee, your supervisor at the group practice will dictate your schedule and the ways in which you carry out your duties. You'll most likely receive some benefits, such as medical insurance, paid holidays and vacation, and perhaps some sort of retirement savings plan. Your employer will pay its share of your Social Security and Medicare taxes, and you'll receive a W4 form to use when filing your state and federal income taxes. Your professional liability coverage may also be provided by the group.

Independent Contractor vs. Employee

Here is a quick summary of the main benefits and drawbacks of working as an independent contractor vs. as an employee:

Independent Contractor Benefits
- Complete control over your practice and the way in which you run it.
- A flexible work schedule that you put together yourself.
- Your choice of where to focus your practice and which clients to accept.

Independent Contractor Drawbacks
- Complete responsibility for all expenses, including taxes and insurance.
- Responsibility for promoting practice and attracting clients.

Employee Benefits

- Employer-provided benefits such as insurance and paid vacations.
- Employer pays a portion of taxes.
- Employer provides clients.

Employee Drawbacks

- Little or no choice in how practice is run.
- Less flexibility in scheduling.
- Less control over how the job is done.

A Warning

The information presented here is very general and always subject to change. It should not be taken as professional advice. An accountant or attorney can give you specific guidance on the difference between independent contractors and employees and how it might apply to a position you're considering. You can also find more information on the Internal Revenue Service website at www.irs.gov/businesses/small/article/0,,id=99921,00.html.

OTHER EMPLOYERS

If you don't want to practice on your own or join a group, you can still earn a salary at the high end of the wage scale by taking a job with a school or government agency. School positions include elementary and secondary schools, community colleges, four-year colleges and universities. Government jobs may be found at the local, county, state and federal levels. Hospitals and social service agencies also pay decent wages, although somewhat lower than their governmental and educational counterparts.

Residential care facilities for substance abuse, mental health and mental retardation tend to be at the low end of the pay scale. They are often used as an entry-level springboard for counselors going through the licensure process who need to earn supervised hours or those who are just starting out in their careers, so they tend to have a high turnover rate.

Some counselors do spend most or all of their careers working at these facilities. They find that the work itself is rewarding enough to compensate for the lower wages. Long-term workers often start in this field during their practicum or internship period. They find it so fulfilling that they stay on in a permanent position once they have graduated and earned their license.

SALARY BREAKDOWN BY EMPLOYER

As of 2006, here are the average annual salaries at various employers, listed by highest to lowest salary, as compiled by the Bureau of Labor Statistics:

Junior Colleges: $59,590
State Government: $51,450

Elementary and Secondary Schools: $49,320
Other Ambulatory Health Care Service Facilities: $48,980
Local Government: $47,420
Offices of Other Health Practitioners: $42,840
Individual and Family Services: $39,240
Outpatient Care Centers: $39,470
Residential Mental Retardation, Mental Health and Substance Abuse Facilities: $31,550

PAY POTENTIAL IN VARIOUS STATES

Your location can also play a major role in how much of a salary you'll earn. If you are willing to relocate, you can boost your earnings substantially. As of 2007, the top paying state for mental health counselors was Montana, where the average annual income was $58,800. This is a difference of almost $30,000 when compared to the lowest paid state (Louisiana, $29,730).

Here is a list of the average state salaries in 2007, including the District of Columbia, listed from highest to lowest salary. These figures come from the Bureau of Labor Statistics:

Montana: $58,800
Nevada: $49,220
Vermont: $48,730
Utah: $46,690
Missouri: $46,230
California: $45,540
Virginia: $45,390
Oregon: $45,210
New Mexico: $44,350
Michigan: $44,090
Washington: $43,860
Wisconsin: $43,110
Minnesota: $42,670
Maine: $42,010
Delaware: $41,340
Ohio: $41,280
New Hampshire: $41,050
Connecticut: $40,950
District of Columbia: $40,420
Wyoming: $40,290
North Carolina: $39,390
Hawaii: $39,320
South Carolina: $39,310
Illinois: $39,270

Arizona: $39,180
Florida: $39,130
New Jersey: $39,070
Texas: $38,590
Oklahoma: $38,550
Maryland: $38,520
Rhode Island: $38,500
Nebraska: $38,420
Indiana: $38,400
Georgia: $38,140
Mississippi: $37,730
Idaho: $37,720
Massachusetts: $37,590
South Dakota: $37,510
West Virginia: $36,770
Arkansas: $36,620
New York: $36,590
Alabama: $36,310
Colorado: $36,180
Kentucky: $35,050
Pennsylvania: $34,570
Kansas: $34,450
Iowa: $34,180
Tennessee: $30,370
Louisiana: $29,730
Alaska - Information not released
North Dakota - Information not released

COST OF LIVING

If you're considering moving to another state to practice counseling because of its higher pay scale, you'll need to do some research first because the cost of living can vary widely between states. For example, in the latter part of 2008 Tennessee had the lowest cost of living in the entire United States. Even though it ranks at the bottom end of wages, the price you'll pay for housing, food and other expenses will also be lower.

If you want to maximize your financial power, choose a state with a good balance between average salary and cost of living. For example, Nevada is a top-paying state, and it also had the fourth lowest cost of living in the United States as of late 2008.

Even within a particular state, living expenses can vary from city to city. To get the latest information for all 50 states and many major cities, visit http://swz.salary.com/CostOfLivingWizard/layouthtmls/coll_statebrief_A.html.

LICENSURE REQUIREMENTS

Currently there is no national counseling license. Each state is free to impose its own requirements. Many of these requirements are similar. Most states require a master's degree, and applicants for licensure must also earn a certain amount of supervised experience, pass an exam, and agree to abide by a code of ethics. There can be some differences, too, so you should research the specific requirements of each state you are considering. A complete list of links to the appropriate licensing boards can be found in the chapter on licensing.

LONG-TERM PROSPECTS

If counseling sounds like it's the right career for you and the wages are acceptable, now is the perfect time to start pursuing that goal. Government statistics show that the mental health field is going through a tremendous growth phase that is expected to last until at least 2016. As of 2006, the Bureau of Labor Statistics (BLS) estimated that there was a total of 630,000 professional counselors working in the United States. The largest chunk of this number was made up of educational, school and vocational counselors (260,000). This was followed by rehabilitation counselors (141,000), mental health counselors (100,000) and substance abuse counselors (83,000). There were also 25,000 marriage and family therapists and 27,000 counselors working in various other fields.

The BLS projects that between 2009 and 2016 the number of openings for trained counselors will exceed the number of students graduating from counseling programs, meaning a high demand for trained professionals. This has the potential to translate into rising salaries and a pick of prime positions.

The BLS also says that overall employment prospects for counselors will increase by 21 percent over the next several years. While this number will vary by specialty, overall it's much higher than projected growth for most other occupations. The BLS attributes this growth to the expansion of available jobs as well as the need to replace people moving out of the field.

Where Is The Highest Growth Potential?

The areas with the highest projected growth are general mental health counseling and marriage and family therapy. Both of those fields are expected to expand by up to 30 percent. For mental health counselors, much of the growth will be driven by the increasing need for services by children and adolescents struggling with emotional disturbances and their families. Many managed care insurance plans are referring such clients to mental health counselors as a more cost-effective alternative to psychiatrists and psychologists.

For marriage and family therapists, demand for their services will continue to boom as more couples and families recognize the need to reach out for help with their conflicts. Seeking mental health counseling is rapidly losing its stigma. Instead, it is coming to be recognized as a valid, healthy and even courageous choice. The client base will expand as the barriers to reaching out for counseling disappear.

Job opportunities for rehabilitation counselors are projected to grow by 23 percent. This rapid expansion will be driven by continued advances in medicine which will allow more people to survive injury or illness and achieve independence with the help of a counselor. Legislation that mandates equal employment rights for people with disabilities will also help to feed the growth as rehabilitation counselors help them transition to the workforce and take advantage of the opportunities created by the law.

The projected growth rate for vocational, educational and school counselors is lower (13 percent), but this is still equivalent to expected job growth in other professions.

CHAPTER SUMMARY

- As of 2006, the Bureau of Labor Statistics (BLS) says that the average salary for a counselor was $47,530. This can vary widely, depending on the workplace and the state of practice.
- Some counselors who work in a group practice are considered employees, while others are classified as independent contractors. There are benefits and drawbacks to each classification.
- According to the BLS, salaries are highest for counselors in private practice and those who work for schools, while the lowest salaries are paid by residential mental retardation, mental health and substance abuse facilities.
- BLS statistics show that as of 2007 counselors in Montana earned the highest average salary ($58,800), while those in Louisiana earned the lowest ($29,730).
- Besides salary, cost of living and licensure requirements should be taken into account when choosing a practice location.
- Overall job opportunities for professional counselors are expected to rise 21 percent through the year 2016 according to the BLS.

SIMILAR PROFESSIONS

The general public often confuses the many job titles and roles that are found in the mental health professions. They use the words "psychiatrist" and "psychologist" interchangeably and think that a counselor or therapist can prescribe antidepressants and other medications. They may believe that a social worker is interchangeable with other counseling classifications. All of these are common misconceptions.

When you're looking at career options, it's important to know the distinctions and characteristics of related jobs. Although this book is centered on becoming a master's level mental health counselor, it's worth taking a look at the other branches of the field to see if one might be more suited to your abilities and preferences.

PSYCHIATRISTS

Psychiatrists are medical doctors (M.D.s) who have chosen the treatment of mental disorders as their specialty in the same way that a podiatrist has chosen to treat ailments related to the feet or an oncologist has chosen to specialize in treating cancer.

Some psychiatrists conduct talk therapy sessions with clients, but overall they approach and treat mental health issues from a medical standpoint. They look for biological causes and influences such as genetics, hormones, brain abnormalities or chemical imbalances. They can prescribe any medications, including psychotropic drugs, and perform medical procedures like electro convulsive therapy (ECT) to treat mental disorders.

Growth Potential

The entire field of medicine is expected to grow by 14 percent through 2016 according to the Bureau of Labor Statistics (BLS), and psychiatric medicine will share in this growth. Research is unlocking the mysteries of brain chemistry and the physical/biological basis for many mental illnesses, and this leads to newer, more effective, drug-based treatments. This trend supports the continued expansion of the psychiatric field.

Earning Potential

Because psychiatrists are medical doctors, they have the highest earning potential of all mental health professionals. According to the BLS, those who have been in practice more than two years earn a median annual salary of $180,000.

Training Requirements

As medical doctors, psychiatrists typically must go through eight years of education beyond high school and up to eight additional years of internship and residency. They are required to be licensed in all 50 states and the District of Columbia. They go through four years of undergraduate school, four years of medical school, and an internship and residency that lasts for several additional years.

In addition to the lengthy time investment, those who are interested in becoming psychiatrists face the highly competitive arena of getting accepted into a medical school and the high cost of tuition if they can earn that coveted acceptance. According to the Association of American Medical Colleges, in 2004 over 80 percent of all medical school graduates, including psychiatrists, were in debt because of their educational expenses. While the high earning potential of this career helps them to pay it off, it can take some time while they find a good work position or build up a solid private practice.

Is Psychiatry The Right Career For You?

If this sounds like a field that might interest you, ask yourself the following questions. The more you answer with a "yes," the more likely it is that psychiatry might be a viable career for you:

- Do you have the academic skills and background to get accepted into medical school?
- Are you wiling to put in the long years of school work, internships and residency before you can begin to practice?
- Do you have the financial resources to support a medical school education or are you willing to take on substantial debt?

Some psychiatrists conduct talk therapy sessions with clients, but overall they approach and treat mental health issues from a medical standpoint.

- Do you tend to take a biological view of mental health issues?

Personal Insight

Dr. Ankur Saraiya, M.D., is a board-certified psychiatrist practicing in New York who chose a career in psychiatry for several reasons. He explains, "I went to medical school without a specific idea of what specialty I wanted to practice. I had a general idea that I liked helping others and I liked the challenge of medical school. I chose psychiatry because it seemed to be the area that would offer a lifelong challenge.

"Other specialties seemed like they would get repetitive. Certainly it takes years to master becoming say, a surgeon, but that's years of doing a lot of the same thing over and over. It takes years to become a skilled psychiatrist too, but you're not just working with a body part. You're working with the whole person and all of their relationships and life history and it can't help but be fascinating."

Dr. Saraiya has found great satisfaction in his career. He says, "The most rewarding part is that I get to directly help improve people's lives every day. I did not realize how important this was until I started hearing from my friends who were lawyers, or bankers, or in some corporate job. Many of them enjoyed their jobs but felt a sense of dissatisfaction that I never knew because this is the only career I've ever had. I often get to work with families and there is no feeling like the one you get when a parent expresses their gratitude to you for helping their child and lets you know that they feel reassured knowing that their son or daughter is in your care."

PSYCHOLOGISTS

Psychologists hold a doctorate degree in psychology, but they are not medical doctors. Their degree might be a Ph.D. (doctor of philosophy who has majored in psychology) or a Psy.D. (doctor of psychology). In general, a Ph.D. degree is more focused on research while a Psy.D. is geared towards practical application in a counseling practice. However, Ph.D.s also learn professional counseling skills to prepare them for direct work with clients and Psy.D.s receive some research training.

Psychologists can conduct therapy sessions, and they can also perform assessment and diagnosis of mental illness and emotional disorders as listed in the Diagnostic and Statistical Manual of Mental Disorders. They provide diagnosis and/ or treatment planning for people who suffer from mental, emotional, or behavioral

Most psychologists cannot prescribe drugs, but there is a growing movement to allow them to prescribe certain psychotropic medications if they receive appropriate training.

problems. A psychologist identifies the problem through clinical and personal history, interviews, testing and assessment. She may provide counseling herself or refer the client to another mental health professional and monitor his progress throughout the treatment process.

Rather than working in a clinical setting, some psychologists focus on research. This may include conducting studies and analyzing the results, developing and evaluating mental health programs, giving presentations at conferences and symposiums, and publishing findings in professional and trade journals.

There are also psychologists who focus on academic careers, teaching undergraduate and graduate psychology classes at colleges and universities. This may be a full-time position, or they may work as adjunct instructors while maintaining a full-time practice or related job.

Most psychologists cannot prescribe drugs, but there is a growing movement to allow them to prescribe certain psychotropic medications if they receive appropriate training. Some states have passed legislation allowing them to do so if they take additional special classes beyond their degree program.

There are several specialties within this field:

Clinical Psychologists

Clinical psychologists usually work in counseling centers, independent or group practices, hospitals, clinics or other settings where they are in direct contact with patients. They work with mentally and emotionally distressed clients and help people cope with issues such as depression or anxiety, personal crisis, losses such as divorce or the death of a loved one, or any other type of mental, emotional or cognitive disturbance. They may provide treatment in individual, family or group sessions.

Some clinical psychologists focus on diagnosis. They interview clients and administer a variety of tests and assessments to pinpoint a disorder or mental illness, and then refer them to appropriate treatment.

Counseling Psychologists

Counseling psychologists are very similar to clinical psychologists. They use interviewing, testing, and other techniques to pinpoint a person's problems. Then they create a treatment plan and conduct counseling sessions with the clients. Typical issues they might tackle include career or work challenges and life stage problems. They might also focus on dealing with the symptoms and effects of a particular mental illness. They work in settings such as individual or group practices, university counseling centers, and inpatient or outpatient facilities.

School Psychologists

School psychologists work with students in elementary and secondary schools. They partner with teachers, parents, and school personnel to create and maintain a healthy learning environment for children. They often address learning and behavioral problems, evaluate existing programs in the school system, and suggest improvements to classroom management strategies. They also evaluate students with disabilities and gifted students to pinpoint the best ways to serve these exceptional youngsters' needs.

Industrial/Organizational Psychologists

Industrial/organizational psychologists apply psychological principles and research methods to the workplace. Their goal is to improve productivity and increase the quality of work life for employees. They are also involved in research on management and marketing problems. They may screen, train, and counsel job applicants, as well as perform organizational development and analysis.

An industrial psychologist often works with management to reorganize the work setting in ways that improve productivity or boost quality of life in the professional environment. Although they may be directly employed by a company, industrial psychologists often work as consultants. In this case, they are brought in by management to solve a particular problem.

Developmental Psychologists

Developmental psychologists study the physiological, cognitive, and social development that takes place throughout the various stages of a person's life. Many of them also may study the effects of developmental disabilities.

Specializations in this field include behavior development during infancy, childhood, and adolescence or the changes that take place during maturity and on through old age. Research in this latter area is helping professionals create ways to support older adults so they can remain independent for as long as possible rather than entering nursing homes or other long-term care facilities.

Social Psychologists

Social psychologists focus on how people interact with others and with the social environment around them. They view interactions in terms of attitude, perception and group behavior. These professionals often work in areas such as organizational consultation, marketing research, systems design, or other fields where they can directly apply their knowledge and findings to developing a plan or course of action.

Research Psychologists

As the name implies, these psychologists conduct research and study the behavior of humans and various experimental animals such as monkeys or rats. Their research may involve topics such as thought, attention, motivation, the learning process, memory, sensory and perceptual processes, effects of substance abuse, and the genetic and neurological factors that affect behavior. They often work in a controlled laboratory setting, but they may conduct field studies as well. They are frequently employed by universities and private research centers, but they may also be found in business, nonprofit, and governmental organizations.

Growth Potential

According to the Bureau of Labor Statistics (BLS), employment for all psychologists is expected to grow 15 percent by 2016. This is due to the increased demand for psychological services in schools, hospitals, social service agencies, mental health centers, substance abuse treatment clinics, consulting firms, and private companies. Job prospects are brightest for psychologists who focus their degree in an applied specialty such as school psychology.

Earning Potential

According to the BLS, psychologists earned a mean annual salary of $68,150 as of 2007. This varied among specialties; for example, school psychologists earned a mean annual salary of $66,040, while those working in private offices earned $81,160 and research psychologists earned $88,830.

Training Requirements

Psychologists typically hold a Doctorate in Psychology (Psy.D.) or Doctor of Philosophy in Psychology (Ph.D.) degree. The Psy.D. is geared towards practical application in a counseling practice, while the Ph.D. focuses more heavily on research in addition to clinical applications of knowledge.

Many people confuse holding a doctorate degree in psychology with actually being a psychologist. The degree alone doesn't legally qualify a person to work as a psychologist, just as a master's degree in counseling doesn't legally qualify a person to practice as a counselor or therapist as soon as they graduate. In order to enter the profession and use the title, you must obtain a state license which may or may not require additional qualifications beyond the degree.

Is Becoming a Psychologist the Right Career For You?

If this field piques your interest, ask yourself the following questions. The more you answer with a "yes," the more likely it is that being a psychologist might be a good fit:

- Do you have the extra years and financial resources to invest in the additional schooling that it takes to earn a doctorate degree?
- Would you enjoy doing testing, assessment and diagnosis rather than focusing only on counseling?
- Would you prefer a career in research rather than interacting directly with clients?
- Are you interested in teaching at the college/university level?

 *Personal Insight*

Patricia Berliner, a psychologist practicing in New York, entered the profession because "I have always loved people and stories, so being a psychologist is the perfect combination.

"It is a privilege to be with people who come to me hurting, fearful, overwhelmed, confused or even just to have someone to talk to and run things by. I am awed by how well some people with overwhelming situations give thanks for being alive and having what they have. I am drawn to them by their openness with me and by the trust they put in me to take them seriously, to keep their confidences and to help them walk into their own paths. It is they who teach me what it means to be an ever-growing human being."

PSYCHIATRIC AND MENTAL HEALTH NURSES

Psychiatric and mental health nursing is a specialty within the broader nursing field. These professionals work with patients who have mental illnesses or issues such as schizophrenia, bipolar disorder, psychosis, depression or dementia. They may also assist in the administration of medical treatments for mental disorders, such as electroconvulsive therapy (ECT).

Psychiatric/mental health nurses work in a variety of settings. One of the most common is on the mental ward of a hospital or in an in-patient facility dedicated to treating mental health or substance abuse issues. They may work exclusively with adults or at a facility that includes or specializes in treating children and adolescents. These nurses are also found in rehabilitation clinics where they can assist with physical needs and help patients deal with the mental and emotional effects of a health crisis or devastating injury.

Nursing homes or other facilities that care for aging adults often employ psychiatric/mental health nurses. Older patients may be dealing with Alzheimer's disease and other forms of dementia. Their special training helps them work effectively with this population and its special challenges.

Some psychiatric/mental health nurses work out in the community, helping people with mental issues to adapt socially and live independently. They may provide in-home services to patients in private residences or those living in group homes.

Psychiatric mental health nurses may also work in the field of forensic psychiatry. This involves the treatment of people who are being detained because they have committed a crime or are considered to be dangerous. Nurses who work with this population typically have a job on a secured ward or in the medical section of a detention facility.

Growth Potential

According to the American Psychiatric Nurses Association (APNA), there is an ongoing shortage of nurses in the United States, and this applies to psychiatric/mental health nurses too. This shortage means that all types of nurses will continue to be in high demand in the job market for the foreseeable future.

Earning Potential

The APNA says that basic-level psychiatric/mental health nurses usually start at an annual salary of $35,000 to $40,000. Pay can be higher, depending on education level, experience, employer, shift worked, and geographic location.

Training Requirements

Psychiatric and mental health nurses receive the same training that is required for a general nursing career. Becoming a registered nurse (RN) requires a two year associate's degree program, a three-year hospital-based diploma program, or a four-year bachelor's degree program. All of these programs prepare a student to take the RN licensing examination after graduation.

To prepare for their specialty, these nurses receive additional training in psychological therapies, building a therapeutic alliance, dealing with challenging behavior, and the administration and effects of psychotropic medication.

The American Nurses Credentialing Center (ANCC) provides certification for psychiatric/mental health nurses. More information, including specific requirements, can be found on their website at www.nursecredentialing.org. The National League for Nursing (NLN) and the American Association of Colleges of Nursing (AACN) both accredit psychiatric/mental health nursing programs. Additional information can be found on their websites at www.nln.org and www.aacn.nche.edu.

If you have a definite interest in nursing, you can enroll in a basic nursing program that provides a rotation in a mental health facility or psychiatric ward. This will give you hands-on experience so you'll know what to expect if you decide to move permanently into psychiatric/mental health nursing.

Professional Organizations for Psychiatric Nurses

The American Psychiatric Nurses Association (APNA) is an organization that is committed to the specialty practice of psychiatric and mental health nursing. Its website is www.apna.org. There may be other professional organizations that you can find through your school, workplace, or colleagues.

Is Psychiatric/Mental Health Nursing the Right Career for You?

If this sounds like an intriguing field, ask yourself the following questions. The more you answer with a "yes," the more likely it is that psychiatric nursing might be a career worth pursuing.

- Does nursing interest you as a career option as much as the mental health field does?
- Would you enjoy caring for both the physical and psychiatric needs of patients?
- Would you like combining medical training with psychology classes?
- Would you enjoy working in a structured hospital environment?
- Do you prefer to be part of a workplace team?

SOCIAL WORKERS

Like counselors, social workers typically have a master's degree (Master of Social Work) and are state licensed professionals. The main difference between these two occupations is the big-picture focus. While social workers might provide talk therapy to their clients, their work often goes beyond that scope and spills over into areas that involve the whole family and outside support systems.

Their duties include helping clients find other resources in addition to counseling. For example, they might guide a troubled family to parenting classes or help a homeless person find a place to live. They might help unemployed clients locate job training programs. They might assist a student with a learning disability and help her parents obtain necessary services to support her academic needs. Social workers often take active roles in social justice issues and strive for societal change.

Many social workers help clients tackle such issues as chronic illness, poverty, drug and other addictions, child and spousal abuse, and homelessness. They often serve as the link for patients between hospitalization and rehabilitation, guiding them in the transition back to a normal and productive life. Some social workers organize and facilitate support groups,

Social workers often take active roles in social justice issues and strive for societal change.

help clients obtain various community services, refer them to other professionals and organizations, and link them up with appropriate programs.

Social workers interview individual clients and their families to assess their physical, social, and psychological needs and formulate an appropriate plan. They also work with civic, religious, and business groups to combat social problems through community-based initiatives. Social workers may specialize in any of the following areas: medical, school, geriatric, family and child welfare, mental health, substance abuse, or adult and juvenile justice.

There are several common sub-specialties within this field:

Child, Family, and School Social Workers

Child, family, and school social workers work with youngsters and their family members in a variety of circumstances. This might include anything from instructing parents in child-raising skills to helping place abused and neglected children into appropriate foster homes. Some of these social workers focus on the older adult population, guiding them to available services and investigating cases of elder abuse.

In a school setting, these social workers deal with common societal problems, such as shyness, self-esteem issues, and bullying. They also partner with teachers and parents to help students who are struggling with learning disabilities, behavior problems and related issues.

Medical and Public Health Social Workers

Medical and public health social workers support clients who are dealing with acute or chronic illnesses. They offer emotional support to people facing ongoing health challenges. These social workers also guide their clients to resources such as classes and support groups related to their condition. For example, they might point a diabetic to a "Living With Diabetes" seminar and a support group made up of others with the same condition.

Mental Health and Substance Abuse Social Workers

Mental health and substance abuse social workers may also be called clinical social workers. Like a mental health counselor, they conduct therapy with clients to help them through a variety of life problems and emotional issues. This may include people struggling with substance abuse/addictions, or their clients might have general problems such as anxiety, depression, or difficulty managing anger.

In addition to working with individual clients, these social workers may teach life skills classes and do community outreach work. Many work in an office setting, but some also venture out into the field to provide in-home services.

Growth Potential

Jobs for social work are expected to grow by 22 percent through 2016 according to the Bureau of Labor Statistics (BLS). The areas with the highest growth potential are those that involve serving the rapidly growing population of aging adults. Job opportunities in rural areas are also expected to boom. Social workers who specialize in working with substance abusers are likely to see a high rate of job growth because courts are increasingly sentencing offenders to treatment programs rather than imprisoning them.

Earning Potential

Social workers earned a mean annual wage of up to $44,670 as of 2007, according to the BLS. This varied by employer and field of practice. For example, social workers in schools earned a mean annual wage of $54,750, while those working in inpatient treatment facilities for substance abusers earned $43,260 and those providing individual and family services earned $39,190.

Is Social Work the Right Career For You?

If this sounds like a field that might interest you, ask yourself the following questions. The more you answer with a "yes," the more likely it is that social work might be the right career choice:

- Do you see your work in terms of the bigger picture?
- Do you feel strongly about social justice issues?
- Would you prefer to make a difference in society as a whole rather than being limited to work with individuals?
- Would you like to provide in-home services and work out in the community rather than staying in an office?

PASTORAL COUNSELORS

Pastoral counselors are trained mental health professionals who also have gone through religious/theological instruction. This allows them to add a spiritual aspect to the counseling they provide. Many ordained ministers, rabbis, priests and other religious leaders provide pastoral counseling services, either separately or as a part of their overall duties.

Growth Potential

According to a 2007 report by the Gallup news service, more than 40 percent of Americans say that they regularly attend church or synagogue services. Twenty-three percent of these attendees say that spiritual growth and guidance is the most important reason for their attendance. Each of these people is a potential client for pastoral counseling.

Many more Americans define themselves as "spiritual but not religious." They too might seek out counseling with a spiritual aspect, particularly from a pastoral counselor who offers a non-denominational approach.

Earning Potential

The pastoral counselors earn an average of $47,990 annually, depending on their workplace and the services they offer. Some pastoral counselors don't earn a separate salary because their counseling duties are part of their overall ministerial work.

Training Requirements

Very few states spell out specific licensing requirements for persons calling themselves "pastoral counselors." A set of professional standards has been laid out by the American Association of Pastoral Counselors (AAPC), an organization that supports counselors in this field. These standards are voluntary, but AAPC members must agree to abide by them

The AAPC dictates that its members who provide pastoral counseling services should meet the following requirements: a bachelor's degree from an accredited college or university; a three-year professional degree from a seminary; and a master's or doctoral degree in the mental health field. Pastoral counselors who adhere to AAPC requirements must also complete post-graduate training which involves a minimum of 1375 hours of supervised clinical experience and 250 hours of direct supervision of that work. More details can be found on the AAPC website at www.aapc.org.

Is Pastoral Counseling the Right Career For You?

If this field sounds appealing, ask yourself the following questions. The more you answer with a "yes," the more likely it is that pastoral counseling might be a good option for you:

- Is religion and/or spirituality an important part of your personal life?
- Would you like to incorporate it into your professional life as well?
- Would you like to affiliate yourself with a church or religious organization?
- Would it be fulfilling to be able to combine your faith and beliefs with your job?

Personal Insight

Sometimes being a counselor can have benefits for a professional as well as for the clients. Stephanie Florman, an ordained reverend/spiritual counselor practicing in New York, entered the field because "I realized that helping others as a counselor would require me to help myself as an individual. I understood that I could not take another to a place that I have not been within myself and that I could not support another in moving through their challenges if I was not willing to meet my own. I decided to become a counselor because my work requires me to continuously strengthen, heal and develop myself."

Stephanie finds her work to be deeply rewarding. She says it helps her to know that "I am living my life's purpose on purpose, feeling that my work with individuals contributes to healing this world as a whole, earning people's trust, receiving my client's story and helping them make connections that create positive changes in their life experience and being constantly reminded of the human spirit and all of its resilience."

LIFE COACHES

Many people don't really know the difference between mental health counselors and life coaches. Counselors treat clients with cognitive, emotional and personality disorders, while life coaches focus on specific life issues and assist clients in creating a plan to achieve clear-cut goals. While counselors often help clients heal wounds from their past, a life coach guides them exclusively in forward movement.

Most coaching clients are psychologically healthy people who simply want to improve their lives in a specified area. Life coaches focus on goal-setting and the steps it takes to achieve a specific outcome. They also guide clients through personal change management, but they don't work directly on alleviating psychological pain. They act as neutral listeners who offer an objective perspective.

According to a survey by the International Coaching Federation (ICF), the most common types of coaching sought by clients are executive coaching, leadership coaching, and life vision and enhancement. There are four common specialties that many coaches choose as a focus. Following is a brief description of each.

Personal Coaching

Personal coaching is sought by individuals looking for help in making decisions or improving their lives, either overall or in designated areas. These many include goal setting, increasing and maintaining motivation, improving academic performance, self care, health and fitness, managing finances, improving interpersonal relationships, becoming more organized or enhancing creativity.

While counselors often help clients heal wounds from their past, a life coach guides them exclusively in forward movement.

115

Career Coaching

Career coaching might involve any aspect of an individual's work life. People seek career coaches to help them become more successful in their current job, weigh career decisions, prepare for and manage a major career change, or make it through transition periods. Career coaches can also assist with bringing work/life balance into kilter.

Corporate Coaching

Corporate coaching is commonly sought by executives and managers who want to improve their skills. They often have a particular focus such as strategic planning, creating or re-engineering a vision, and conducting effective performance reviews. Corporate coaches may also be employed by companies to guide initiatives such as team building and training internal coaches.

Small Business Coaching

Small business coaching is often sought by entrepreneurs who want to develop and hone the necessary skills for starting and running a successful enterprise. They may need assistance with goal setting, creating a vision, maintaining their focus, and staying on track. Coaches can also help people who are weighing whether or not they want to leave their current job to start a business. They can lead uncertain clients through an objective reality test to make the best decision.

Growth Potential

Life coaching is a rapidly growing profession. The ICF estimates that there are 10,000 life coaches in the United States, a 300 percent increase since 2000. Overall, life coaching was estimated to be a $1.5 billion global industry as of 2006, and its expansion is continuing unabated.

Earning Potential

In a 2006 study the ICF reported that full-time life coaches earned an average annual salary of $82,671. Coaches working part time earned an average of $26,150.

Training Requirements

At present most states don't require a license to practice as a life coach, so there are no legal standards for education and training. A 2006 study by the ICF revealed that 53 percent of professional life coaches had earned a graduate degree.

To earn a Professional Certified Coach (PCC) credential from the ICF, applicants must complete an approved training program with a minimum of

125 hours of coach-specific training. Their studies must also cover the ICF core competencies and code of ethics. The training program also requires six observed coaching sessions and with an experienced coach watching and evaluating and a comprehensive final exam. Also required is the accumulation of a minimum of 750 coaching experience hours, and the applicant must have at least 25 clients.

In addition to the ICF, there are six other self-appointed accreditation groups for individual life coaches and/or schools/training programs: the International Coaching Council (ICC), the International Association of Coaching (IAC), the Certified Coaches Federation (CCF), the European Coaching Institute (ECI) and the International Guild of Coaches (IGC). Each has their own requirements for credentialing, which can be found on the websites listed in the Resources section at the end of this book. All of these groups are privately owned, and there is currently no independent body to oversee them.

Is Life Coaching the Right Career For You?

If this sounds like an appealing line of work, ask yourself the following questions. The more you answer with a "yes," the more likely it is that life coaching might be a fulfilling career choice:

- Would you prefer a career that is similar to counseling but requires less of a training investment?
- Would you prefer to help clients make immediate life changes rather than delve deeply into issues?
- Do you have a dynamic personality?
- Are you very goal-oriented and good at motivating others?

 *Personal Insight*

Sara Holliday, a licensed marriage and family therapist who also works as a life and fitness coach, finds her coaching work to be very fulfilling. "I enjoy when clients have 'ahhh hah' moments and when clients take responsibility for the turmoil they have and then learn how to take action to make their lives better in every aspect...relationships, health and balance," she says.

Sara sees her role as a guide, "helping clients discover the answer within themselves. I ask questions and reflect back what I hear which guides them to their own resolution."

As a holistic health practitioner, Sara finds that coaching often leads clients to confront deeper issues. She explains, "Most commonly my female clients come for weight issues, but after deeper discussion there are often relationship issues and feeling overwhelmed, disconnected and out of balance."

HOLISTIC PRACTITIONERS

Many professionals in mental health related fields take a holistic approach. This means that they acknowledge the interrelationship of mind, body and spirit and how this connection affects a client's emotional state.

Many common emotional issues manifest themselves with physical symptoms. For example, anxiety often leads to difficulty breathing, tightness in the chest, and a feeling of being disconnected. Stress can show itself via headaches and muscle tightness.

Holistic practitioners combine traditional therapeutic or coaching techniques with other methods designed to treat the whole person. These may includes meditation, Reiki, energy work, or body work. In addition to their primary professional training, they take classes or seminars related to the complementary technique.

The New England Association of Holistic Counselors (NEHCA) defines a holistic counselor as a professional counselor who meets a specific set of criteria. These are listed on the NEHCA website at www.nehcaweb.org. In summary, they describe a holistic counselor as someone who:

• Has earned a master's degree or higher from an accredited college or university
• Has been trained in the mental health area and also in holistic principles and skills
• Sees the therapeutic process as a partnership between the client and counselor
• Acknowledges the client's own ability to heal, become whole, and find meaning and purpose
• Helps the client achieve awareness, expression and integration of mind, body and spirit
• Guides clients on the path of balance even when they are faced with paradox and uncertainty
• Integrates the fruits of his or her personal journey of growth to enhance the counseling relationship
• Practices on variety of levels: personal, interpersonal, family, group, organizational, or global
• Adheres to a specified code of ethics for the profession

The NEHCA says that holistic principles are based on the recognition that:
• The universe is a whole that is made up of various interrelated parts and systems. These include individuals, groups, and organizations.
• All of these various systems are self-organizing, self-maintaining, self-healing, and self transcending.

- Entities are made up of body, mind, emotions, spirit, environment, and the roles played within relationships.
- Balance is necessary to achieve and maintain wellness.
- Healing is something that comes from within and happens in community.
- Holistic approaches are both viable and effective. They are complementary to conventional methods rather than a replacement.
- Holistic practitioners should always provide their services skillfully, respectfully, and ethically.

CHAPTER SUMMARY

- If you're considering professional counseling as your career, you should also look at related fields.
- Similar fields include psychiatry, psychology, psychiatric/mental health nursing, social work, pastoral counseling, and life coaching.
- Some of these fields require a state license to practice. Others have voluntary certification or other credentials offered through professional organizations.
- Some counselors combine holistic methods with their traditional work and take classes in complementary methods such as Reiki and body work.

ARE YOU WILLING TO MAKE THE INVESTMENT?

Even though the outlook for salary and job availability for counselors is very positive, it's not a profession that you can walk into without a significant investment. You must be prepared to earn a graduate degree, including an unpaid practicum/internship that averages 100 hours, and pay all the expenses for your education, including tuition, books, and supplies. Then, depending on the state in which you'll be practicing, you'll most likely have to put time and effort into the licensure process. This usually means earning supervised work hours and taking a comprehensive exam before you receive your full licensure. The exam will require preparation and payment of a fee. When you've finally earned your license, you'll have to earn continuing education units (CEUs) in order to renew it.

If you really believe that counseling might be your best career option, you need to be prepared to make these investments. Let's look at what this entails in greater depth.

TIME INVESTMENT

The time investment required to become a counselor encompasses mainly two parts: a college education that results in a master's degree and the additional time required to earn supervised experience as required by most state licensure boards. There may be additional time and financial commitments as you renew your license and earn the CEUs that many states require to do so.

Schooling

To become a mental health counselor or work in any of the related specialties, you'll need to have a master's degree. If you are able to attend school full-time, this means investing an average of four years of undergraduate work and two additional years of graduate study. If you're limited to part-time schooling, this timeframe will increase exponentially. You may be able to decrease the calendar time by taking a higher class load, but you'll still be putting in the same hours overall.

The master's degree typically consists of a full slate of classroom work, combined with gaining unpaid work experience out in the field. All quality programs will have a practicum requirement that entails volunteering in a supervised counseling position for a certain number of hours. Even though you won't be getting paid, the process is still similar to finding a permanent job. You'll have to search for potential positions, apply for them, and go through an interview process. Then you'll have to put together a schedule that allows you to attend classes while still completing the required number of work hours.

If you're holding a job to help pay your school expenses or if you're an adult who is attending college while also working full or part-time, it will be a special challenge. You'll be working your practicum and internship around your regular employment and juggling other responsibilities.

Licensure

Once you have earned your degree, virtually every state will require you to earn a specified amount of supervised work experience before you are eligible for full licensure. You may also have to undergo additional state-mandated training that is separate from your degree program. For example, in the state of Florida, to qualify for a mental health counseling license you must take courses in laws and rules and the prevention of medical errors from a state-approved provider.

When you have earned your license, you will be required to renew it regularly. This may entail earning a certain number of CEUs by taking additional classes and providing documentation with your renewal application.

The term "continuing education units" is in the public domain, so any organization can offer CEUs without regulation or approval of an accrediting body. When earning CEUs for your license renewal, make sure to take your classes from a state-approved provider. That is the only way to ensure that you'll fulfill your state's requirements.

MONETARY INVESTMENT

Your college education is the biggest financial expense on the road to becoming a counselor. According to the not-for-profit College Board, an association composed of more than 5,400 colleges, universities, and other educational organizations, for the 2008/2009 school year the cost of a private four year college averages $25,143, while a public four year institution averages $6,585. You can find the most up-to-date statistics on their website at www.collegeboard.com. Tuition accounts for a major chunk, but there are many other costs, such as fees, books, supplies, and living expenses that boost the bill even more. In the following sections, we'll look at each of the school-related expenses in a little more detail.

Tuition

Tuition is the actual cost of your classes, which is usually assessed as a per credit-hour cost. If you haven't already earned any transferable college credits, you'll have to pay for six years worth of classes. This includes four years to earn your bachelor's degree and two years to earn your master's degree.

If you've earned college credits in the past that can be transferred to your current program, this will offset some of the expense. Some high schools allow students to take advanced placement courses through which they can earn college credit. Adults may have taken college classes previously, even if they didn't earn a degree. If you have credits that may be transferable, submit your transcripts or other documentation to the Admissions Office of the colleges you're considering. They can evaluate your past work and let you know how much will transfer.

Students can also take tests through the College-Level Examination Program (CLEP) to earn college credit for their pre-existing knowledge. Taking the exam costs far less than taking a course. There are over 30 exams available on a wide variety of topics. Details can be found at www.collegeboard.com/student/testing/clep/about.html. Before taking any of the CLEP exams, check with prospective colleges to find out their acceptance policy. Almost 3000 schools will give credit through these exams, but each has its own restrictions and limitations as to how many credits they will accept.

Tuition rates typically increase by five to eight percent a year. You don't lock in the current tuition rate when you enroll in school, so you'll need to be prepared for a continually increasing expense. If you are still in high school or would like to estimate the cost of graduate school when you have completed your bachelor's degree, the FinAid website offers a tuition estimator calculator. You can put in the current tuition cost at your schools of interest and the number of years until you'll matriculate and it will automatically estimate the cost at various interest rates. The calculator can be found at www.finaid.org/calculators/costprojector.phtml.

You may be able to lower your tuition outlay by attending a state college instead of a private institution. Earning your degree online can also be a cost effective alternative, since taking internet classes usually costs less than attending school in a bricks-and-mortar classroom. Still, even the least expensive degree programs will run into thousands of dollars.

If you are fortunate enough to qualify for a scholarship or grant, you can partially or totally offset the cost of your education. If not, you'll have to pay the entire amount out-of-pocket or defer repayment through student loans. Financial aid is discussed in more detail later in this chapter.

Books

Most classes require at least one textbook, and some might use more than one volume. College texts can easily cost over $100, so this expense adds up quickly. Purchasing brand-new books from the on-campus bookstore is usually the most expensive option. Some bookstores carry used editions at a discounted price. You can often find steep discounts on both new and used books through internet stores and auction sites. A quick Google search will let you comparison shop online. You may also be able to buy cheap used books from classmates in the same program.

There are some books that you might want to keep as a reference when the class is over. This will be particularly true in your graduate program, when the classes are closely focused on information and techniques you'll be applying directly in your counseling career. For example, the Diagnostic and Statistical Manual of Mental Disorders is often required for graduate classes in psychopathology and diagnosis. It's also a standard volume in the library of virtually any practicing mental health professional. You may also want to keep books about specific therapeutic strategies and treatment plans that you will be using in your practice.

But there will be many other books that you don't plan to ever open again once you complete the class. Recoup some of the cost by selling them to a classmate, your college bookstore, or an online site that buys used texts.

Supplies

Attending college requires an assortment of supplies, such as pens, paper, and notebooks. These many sound minor until you tally up the total over the course of multiple years. Most students also use a computer and printer to do their homework assignments, and an internet connection is a virtual necessity for research. If you don't have your own computer, you may be able to use one at your school or in the public library, but this can be very inconvenient. At some point you'll probably want to invest in your own equipment and internet connection.

Fees

In addition to tuition, many colleges tack a variety of fees onto your bill. They go by a variety of names, such as registration fees, library fees, technology fees, activity fees, and parking fees, but they all share two common features: they are non-negotiable, and you'll have to pay some of them every semester. When you're comparing colleges, be sure to get a list of the relevant fees and add it into your expected costs to get a more accurate picture of the total bill.

Room and Board

If you're attending an out-of-town school, you'll have to pay for a place to live, food, and other day to day expenses. Weigh the cost of dormitories vs. living off campus to see which one is the least expensive option. Some colleges offer all-inclusive packages that include your dorm room and daily meals. This allows you to have fixed expenses rather than dealing with a variable food budget. If you live on campus, you eliminate travel expenses and have easy access to the library, computer lab, and other resources.

FINANCIAL AID

Many students try to offset the cost of their college education by applying for financial aid. As tuition costs increase at a faster pace than income levels, the need for assistance continues to rise. In 2008, the government reported that the number of applications for aid increased by 17 percent.

There are three major types of financial assistance:

- ***Federal Aid.*** This encompasses grants and loans given by the federal government. Much of this aid is need-based, meaning that students must fall within certain income guidelines in order to qualify.

Students can easily find out whether they are eligible for aid from the government, and how much they might receive, through the Free Application for Federal Student Aid (FAFSA). Filling out this application online will let a student assess whether she might be able to get grants, subsidized loans, or some combination of assistance. The application can be filled out by visiting the FAFSA website at www.fafsa.ed.gov.

- ***Grant Aid.*** This comes from a wide variety of sources. It may be offered by the federal government, state governments, employers, professional organizations, and fraternal organizations. Often it is funded by the colleges and universities themselves. A grant is a "gift" of money that you never have to repay.

As tuition costs increase at a faster pace than income levels, the need for assistance continues to rise.

- **Scholarship Aid.** Some students qualify for a partial or full scholarship based on their academic performance. Many state and public colleges and universities offer financial aid packages to students who achieve high scores on the ACT, SAT, or PSAT tests. Students who are named as National Merit Scholars, National Achievement Scholars or National Hispanic Scholars may be eligible for scholarship money as a result of earning these honors.

Scholarships may also be awarded for athletic ability or another talent, such as debating or playing a musical instrument. In order to maintain a talent-based scholarship, you may need to meet ongoing requirements such as participating in a certain sport or activity, and maintaining a specific grade point average. Some scholarships are handed out strictly based on financial need. If you fall within certain income guidelines, you will qualify regardless of most other factors.

Depending on the specific counseling field you plan to enter, related scholarship money may be available. For example, in the field of rehabilitation counseling the U.S. Department of Education Rehabilitation Services Administration funds a scholarship that is awarded to students who are willing to provide services in exchange for the tuition money. The Geriatric Social Work Initiative sponsors awards and fellowships for students who plan to pursue a career in geriatric counseling.

Professional organizations often provide scholarships and awards too. For example, both the American Association for Marriage and Family Therapy and the American School Counselor Association offer scholarships to students who plan to enter those two fields.

The financial aid office at your college of choice may be able to point you toward many of these scholarship opportunities and alert you to others. You can also research professional and government agencies yourself through websites such as www.collegescholarships.org and http://apps.collegeboard.com/cbsearch_ss/welcome.jsp.

Loans

Loans can remove the immediate pressure of paying for your education. You'll get the money you need up front, and you can use it to pay for your tuition, books, supplies and other expenses. Just don't get lulled into a false sense of security; that money will have to be paid back! You might not have to start repayment until you're done with school, but when you enter the working world you'll have a debt hanging over your head.

Loan repayment can be a burden to anyone entering a new career. Counselors face a because they don't gain full licensure in most states until they've completed a specified amount of supervised experience. While they are paid for this work, their earning potential is lower until they get their license.

Don't Default!

If you default on student loans, you can face some serious consequences. These may include:

- Garnishment of your wages. The debtor may be able to claim up to 15 percent of your disposable income, and it will be taken directly from your paycheck.
- Tax refund offsets. One of the most popular ways for the government to collect on defaulted student loans is through the Internal Revenue Service (IRS). Your refund can be offset every year until the loan is paid in full.
- Federal benefit offsets. If you receive certain types of federal benefit payments such as Social Security retirement or disability income, the government can claim up to 15 percent to go towards loan repayment. Supplemental Security Income is exempt, and there are certain limitations on the amount that can be taken from other types of federal benefits.
- Lawsuits. Both the government and private lenders can file a lawsuit to force you to pay your student loans. There is no statute of limitations, so you run the risk of being sued indefinitely if you default on this type of debt.

The National Consumer Law Center's Student Loan Borrower Assistance website has more information on student loans and related payment and collection policies. You can find this information at www.studentloan-borrowerassistance.org.

Types of Loans

There are three main types of loans to finance your education: student loans, parent loans and private (or alternative) student loans. Each has its own benefits and drawbacks, as discussed in the following sections.

Student Loans

Student loans are provided by, and sometimes subsidized by, the United States government. The two main student loan programs are the Federal Stafford Loan and the Perkins Loan.

Any student, regardless of income, qualifies for an unsubsidized Federal Stafford Loan. This program offers competitive interest rates and deferred payment programs that allow you to put off repayment until after graduation.

If you meet certain income guidelines, you may be eligible for a subsidized Federal Stafford Loan. Under this program, the government makes a contribution by paying the interest while you are in school.

The Perkins Loan is a federal program that is limited to students who have financial need. The government provides funds to schools, who then act as the lender to qualified recipients.

The first step in applying for a government loan is to fill out the Free Application for Federal Student Aid (FAFSA), just as you would to determine your eligibility for grants and scholarships. If you are interested in either of these loan programs, complete this application to find out whether you qualify for this assistance along with other types of aid.

Parent Loans

The name "Parent Loan" is a bit of a misnomer, since these loans can also be taken out directly by certain students. If you are still a dependent, your parents can take out loans to supplement any financial aid you will be receiving. The Parent Loan for Undergraduate Students (PLUS) allows them to borrow funds to cover any costs that are not already included in your financial aid package, up to the full cost of attendance.

Graduate and professional students can borrow money for their own schooling through the PLUS program without involving their parents. In order to participate, they must complete the FAFSA and max out their Stafford Loans first.

Private Loans

Private loans, which are also called alternative education loans, can be used to fill in the gap between the cost of your schooling and the amount you're able to borrow through government programs. Because these loans are provided by private lenders, you don't have to submit the FAFSA to apply. Your eligibility will be dependent on your income and credit score, much like a traditional house or car loan.

POST-GRADUATION INTERNSHIP

Once you've earned your degree, you'll be required to earn additional supervised hours as a part of the state licensure process. Many states will issue a provisional license or some type of professional registration while you complete the required hours. Because you are not fully licensed, you will most likely have to take an entry level position that doesn't pay as much as you'll earn as a licensed professional. If necessary, you must be prepared to live on a tight budget or supplement your income with another job during this period.

OTHER EXPENSES

Depending on your employer, you may also have to pay your own license renewal fees and foot the bill for professional liability insurance and continuing education. If you want to join professional organizations, you will probably have to pay for your own membership, although some employers will subsidize at least part of the cost. If you decide to go into private practice, you'll always be responsible for all of these expenses, as well as your own medical insurance and the overhead and ongoing costs of maintaining an office, advertising, and everything else associated with running your own business.

CHAPTER SUMMARY

- Becoming a professional counselor involves a commitment in time that includes six years of college and additional supervised experience to get a state license.
- Becoming a professional counselor involves a monetary commitment to pay for the necessary schooling and related items such as books, supplies, room and board; expenses involved in the licensure process; and ongoing business expenses.
- Educational expenses may be offset through financial aid programs such as grants and scholarships. Those who are not eligible may be able to get student loans.

SPECIAL CHALLENGES FOR ADULTS

If you decide to pursue a counseling career as an adult, you'll face some special challenges. You might not have been able to go to college directly after graduation. You may already have a job, but you want to make a career change. Or perhaps you've never been in the workforce at all, but your life circumstances have changed and you're ready to tackle a degree and professional challenge. No matter what your individual circumstances, it's going to be quite different than going to college directly after high school and preparing for a career at the traditional age.

HOW LONG WILL IT TAKE?

The amount of time it will take you to get your degree and become a counselor depends on many factors. If you already have an associate's or bachelor's degree and can transfer most or all of the credits to a graduate school, you'll cut two to four years or more off the educational timeframe. Even if you didn't earn a degree but took some general college classes, you may be able to transfer them. If you're starting from scratch, you're looking at a minimum of six years of school if you're able to attend full time. This breaks down into four years of full-time study to earn a bachelor's degree and an additional two years to earn a master's.

The National Center for Education Statistics says that 75 percent of adults attending college hold a full or part-time job during their enrollment. If you're going to be fitting your studies around a job and/or family responsibilities, you may be forced to take classes on a part-time basis to allow adequate time for studying and homework. This will increase your school time proportionately.

Your degree program will include an unpaid practicum/internship which will require time outside the classroom. Once you graduate, you'll have to gain one to two years of additional supervised work experience in order to earn a state license. If you don't meet the minimum number of hours required by your state's licensure board, that period will stretch out until you do.

At the bare minimum, if you start your college education from scratch, attend classes full- time, and live in a state where you can fulfill your work-hour requirements in a year, you'll be investing seven years in order to become a licensed professional counselor. Make sure you are fully prepared to make this long-term commitment before you initiate the process.

YOU'RE NOT ALONE

According to the U. S. Department of Education National Center for Education Statistics (NCES), the number of young students has been growing more rapidly than the number of adults attending college, but this pattern is expected to change. Between 1990 and 2005, the enrollment of students under age 25 increased by 33 percent, while enrollment of those age 25 and over rose by 18 percent. From 2005 to 2016, NCES projects a significant shift in those figures. They foresee a rise of only 15 percent in enrollments of students under 25; while there will be a rise of 21 percent in enrollments of people age 25 and over.

Among mature students, the age group with the highest enrollment is age 35 and over. In 2007 there were 3086 adults in this age group enrolled in U.S. colleges and universities, and by 2016 that number is projected to climb to 3319. In contrast, there were 2533 enrollees between 25 to 29 years old, with that number projected to increase to 3168 by 2016. The lowest represented age group was adults between the ages of 30 to 34, with 1337 students enrolled in 2007 and an expected increase to 1741 by 2016.

HELP FOR ADULT STUDENTS

Colleges and universities recognize that adult learners represent a significant group of students with their own special needs. Many have created programs that cater to returning adults. These may include some or all of the following:

- Condensed/accelerated classes that allow for faster degree completion
- Evening and weekend classes
- Online classes
- College credits awarded based on work or life experience
- Satellite locations in convenient settings rather than requiring travel to a campus.
- Counseling services geared to adult learners
- Support groups, study groups and networking opportunities for adult learners

- Direct billing arrangements with companies that offer tuition assistance to employees
- Age-restricted scholarships

When identifying potential schools, an accredited school and counseling program should be your first consideration. Once you've narrowed down your list to accredited schools and programs, make it a special point to find out which ones offer special support and benefits for adult students. This should help you narrow down your list and make your final decision a little easier.

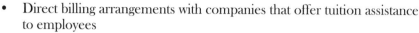

Personal Insight

Rhonda Loft, LMFT, a marriage and family therapist in Connecticut, returned to college at the age of 39 to pursue her counseling degree. She had an undergraduate degree in biology and was working in the electronics field when she decided to take the plunge. She was friends with a psychologist whose stories about life in the mental health field convinced Rhonda to make a career change.

She says, "I think part of it was creating a challenge for myself. Could I take one class and do well? After I got a taste of the courses, the idea of being a professional and getting real satisfaction from a career kept me going."

With a ten-year-old son, she says that the hardest part was "balancing taking care of my family and finding time for studying/term papers." She had to make changes in their routine, like not having dinner together every night and changing vacation plans to accommodate classes, but her husband and family gave her a strong base of support.

It wasn't only the school/family juggling act that had Rhonda a bit worried. She was also worried about being the oldest student in class. She says, "As it turned out I was right in the middle. There was a 70 year old returning to school and 'kids' who had just graduated from college."

She says that the sacrifices were well worth the investment: "I knew it the first time I met with a client and felt that I helped someone make a significant change in their life." She also feels it in "creating what one of my former clients, who decided to become a therapist himself after our work, used to call the 'magic'." Returning to school gave her the tools to create that magic for clients and to be an inspiration to others.

ONLINE SCHOOLS

While many traditional colleges offer internet classes in addition to their regular program, some schools offer degrees that can be earned completely online. These best of these schools offer the same quality of education that you'd receive on a traditional campus, and they are accredited by the same agencies that approve in-person schools.

Online universities are a viable option for older adult students for several reasons:

- They have flexible schedules that can easily be worked around other responsibilities.
- The work is done at home, eliminating travel time and expenses. This means more time can be used directly for schoolwork.
- Students can work at their own pace, allowing them to complete their degree more quickly if they are sufficiently motivated.
- They are often less expensive, which eases the burden for adults who are paying out of pocket because they were unable to get financial aid.

Jo is a good example of someone for whom an online degree program is ideal. She works afternoons and has two young children. They live in a rural area with no major colleges or universities within reasonable driving distance.

By enrolling in an accredited online counseling program, Jo was able to link up with a quality school without being limited by her location. Her university has an online library with databases that put major psychology journals at her fingertips. She downloads articles to conduct research and uploads schoolwork for instructor review. She interacts with her fellow students through a forum and live chat rooms.

Because her house is chaotic until she puts her children to bed, Jo usually works on her assignments late at night. She enjoys being able to fit them around her schedule and family responsibilities. Even though she was able to get a student loan to cover her tuition, she appreciates the fact that her online classes cost lest than comparable classes at a traditional school. This means her repayment amount won't be quite as intimidating when she graduates.

FINANCIAL AID FOR ADULT STUDENTS

While getting scholarships and grants can be a challenge for any student, regardless of age, adult learners often face some special obstacles. Many scholarships are limited to graduating seniors or specifically exclude adults who are transferring community college credits. Scholarships are often restricted to full time students only, which means that adults who are forced to take classes part time due to other life responsibilities are not eligible.

Scholarships and grants tend to be need-based. They use an applicant's income to determine her eligibility. Adult students are often working full-time and may also have a working spouse. Unfortunately, this may render them ineligible for most types of aid based on traditional need guidelines, even though they many have higher household and child-rearing expenses.

This doesn't mean that it's impossible for an adult student to find financial assistance. It just makes the search more difficult. If they are persistent, adults may be able to find money for college through an employer's tuition assistance or scholarship program; scholarships offered by professional organizations; national scholarships aimed specifically at adult learners; and federal or private loans.

Scholarships

According to FinAid, a comprehensive source of online financial aid information, as of 2008 the The FastWeb scholarship database included more than 230 awards with a minimum age restriction of 25 and more than 50 awards that have a minimum age restriction of 30.

Often there are other restrictions on these scholarships, such as being offered exclusively to women or single parents. As an example, the Talbot Women's Scholarship Fund awards a total of $100,000 each year to women entering college at least 10 years after earning their high school diploma or GED. Although these scholarships consider financial need, they are also based on the applicant's achievements so successful women may still qualify. The Royal Neighbors of America offers two scholarships specifically for women age 35 or older, and the Business and Professional Women's Foundation has a career advancement scholarship for women age 25 or older who have a clear career plan and are financially needy.

Some universities have their own programs that offer scholarship money to adult students. Check with the financial aid office of each school you're considering. Their financial aid program just might be a deciding factor in your ultimate choice.

Loans

Adults can also get student loans through federal or private programs. The unsubsidized Stafford Loan does not have any income requirements, and repayment can be deferred until after a student's graduation no matter what their age. Private programs are based on an applicant's credit score, so a high income level is a plus in qualifying for a private student loan.

Tuition Reimbursement Programs

Many employers offer tuition reimbursement programs to encourage their employees to start or complete a college education. Some companies will pay a certain percentage of the cost, while others may foot the entire bill. The program may be limited to tuition costs only, or it may include books, fees, and other expenses.

Most employer-based programs have some restrictions. They may require the classes or degree to have direct on-the-job application in order to be reimbursable. Participants are usually required to maintain a certain grade point average, and they must commit to staying with the employer for a certain length of time after their last class.

Some companies pay the money upfront, while others reimburse the employee after she successfully completes the class. In some areas, colleges partner with major employers to offer direct billing programs as a convenience to participating employees.

As of 2008, tuition reimbursement is exempt from taxes up to a total of $5250. The exemption runs through 2010, although it may be extended by Congress. Check with your company's human resources department and the Internal Revenue Service to get the most current information.

ARE YOU READY FOR THE COMMITMENT?

If you are an adult considering a return to school to earn your counseling degree, ask yourself the following questions:

- *Can I fit the schooling comfortably around my other responsibilities?* The key word is "comfortably". Many people take on more than they can realistically juggle, then buckle under the stress. Tally up all your responsibilities such as work, family and outside activities. Where will school fit in? Will you have to curtail other aspects of your life to make it fit? You might find yourself turning down social invitations or even missing your daughter's soccer game or your son's band concert. Are you willing to make those sacrifices?

- *Am I willing to commit the time and effort?* You have to be prepared to focus on your schoolwork, even at the expense of other activities. This often means making sacrifices such as limited family time or turning down a promotion at work that would mean longer hours. Can you give up things in the short term and focus on the long- term gain?

- *What will this achievement mean to me?* Adults usually enroll in college to study for a new career, but this may not be the only impetus. Will earning your degree give you personal fulfillment as well as open up new professional doors? Perhaps you wanted to earn your degree earlier, but life got in the way. You might not have been able to afford it, or you got a job offer that was just too good to pass up, or you fell in love and started a family early. Would returning to school allow you to realize that long-delayed dream? The more reasons you can pinpoint, the more easily you'll be able to maintain your motivation.

- *How will I handle stress?* School itself is inherently stressful as you complete a mountain of papers and other assignments, cram for exams, and struggle to maintain good grades. Add work and family responsibilities on top of that and your stress level is sure to skyrocket. You need to create a stress management plan before you start school and be committed to using it. Know how you will handle it if the stress starts impeding your life and how you will recognize early warning signs so you can take steps before it becomes unmanageable.

Some examples of stress management strategies might be: saving vacation days so you can take a day off to study for your final exams; scheduling study time each night and getting an agreement from your other family members not to disturb you during that time; scheduling self-care activities such as a pedicure or a long bubble bath to give you a break from schoolwork and other stressors; and taking a lighter class load if your school schedule turns out to be too overwhelming.

- ***Do I have a good support system?*** If you have a family, they need to be supportive of your efforts. No matter how carefully you try to balance school with other responsibilities, there is bound to be some spillover. This will be much less stressful if you're surrounded by an understanding family network. Build your outside support system too. Friends and co-workers can be an excellent source of support. If they know about your juggling act, they'll be more understanding if you're snappish or stressed out at times and they can provide encouragement and an ear to vent when needed.

- ***Does the financial commitment fit into the family budget?*** Paying for college can be a struggle, especially if it's all coming out of pocket. You need to be sure that you can afford tuition and other expenses on your household income. Is your partner's job secure? What about yours if you're planning to continue working while you go to school? You should have an emergency plan for how you would handle a job loss or other major, unexpected financial blow. For example, you might open a new credit card account or get a line of home equity credit with the understanding that it won't be used except in extreme emergencies.

Personal Insight

FROM THE AUTHOR: I earned my graduate degree as an adult returning to school after a ten-year absence. I had earned an associate's degree right after high school, then went to work full time in corporate communications and training. I had always wanted to be a counselor, but I couldn't afford to pursue it. Even though I enjoyed my job, I never gave up that dream.

My employer started a tuition reimbursement program which allowed me to go back to college. I earned a bachelor's degree with a double major in human resources and psychology and the company footed the bill. They agreed to pay for my master's degree, too, if I chose the industrial psychology track in the counseling program.

I worked full-time throughout my bachelor's and master's programs and based my choice of schools on proximity to my workplace, availability of evening classes, and willingness to bill my company directly for tuition.

To earn my degrees more quickly, I took some of my classes through the university's adult education program. It offered an accelerated schedule with classes that met every day, even on holidays. I also took some self-paced classes; at the time, the internet wasn't yet in widespread use for distance learning, so this meant viewing a series of videotapes and completing related assignments.

Earning my degree while working full time was a definite commitment. I put many other areas of my life on hold so I could devote my spare time to studying. My husband was wonderfully supportive, but it was still a very stressful time in my life. I managed to get through it by staying focused on the long-term reward.

The most challenging part of my schooling was the period in which I completed my master's practicum. Not only was I working full time during the day and attending classes in the evening, but I also had to shoehorn in unpaid counseling work and supervision session. I did my internship at a social service agency that offered very flexible work hours.

I knew it was all worthwhile when I finally marched up onto the stage, feeling awkward in my robe and tassel, and accepted my master's degree. I had returned to school in 1995, completed the remaining two years of my bachelor's degree by 1997, and completed my graduate studies in 2000. Not only did I have a sense of academic accomplishment, but I also knew that I'd proven my ability to juggle work, family, and school. My original goal of becoming a counselor might have been delayed, but it was never forgotten, and now I had taken a major step towards turning it into reality.

CHAPTER SUMMARY

- Adults face special challenges when they choose to pursue a counseling career. This includes juggling work/family/personal responsibilities with the required schooling and internship hours.
- Many colleges and universities have special programs geared for adult learners. These may include flexible schedules, accelerated classes, support groups, and credits awarded for work or life experience.
- Online schools are a good alternative for many adult learners because of their flexibility and lower cost.
- Although finding scholarships and grants may be difficult, there are some that are exclusively offered to adult students.
- Some companies offer tuition reimbursement programs for their employees, which can be a good resource for adult students.
- Adults who are interested in a counseling career must carefully consider how they'll fit the responsibilities into their current work and family life and make a concrete plan.

THE DOWNSIDE OF BEING A COUNSELOR

On the surface, being a counselor might sound like a rewarding career with very little on the negative side. In an ideal world, every client who came through your office door would be highly motivated and ready to do the necessary work to conquer their problems. You'd give them the proper tools for positive change, which they would implement immediately. With your guidance, their issues would soon be resolved and they'd live happily ever after while you basked in the glow of another job well done.

Unfortunately, in the real world success is often overshadowed by frustration. Instead of being motivated, many clients will be resistant when they enter counseling. They may not be seeing you by choice; many are pressured into seeking help by other family members, school officials, their boss or another person in a position of power. They may even have been ordered into treatment by a judge under the threat of imprisonment. Under those circumstances, they may not be willing to acknowledge the need for help, let alone cooperate with you and embrace the tools needed for change. Instead, they will quickly drop out of treatment or bide their time until they've fulfilled the court order.

As a counselor, you must be prepared to depersonalize from the parts of your job over which you have no control. Because you are working with a wide variety of people, each of whom has an issue and a variable level of willingness and motivation, you can't guarantee the outcome of the therapeutic relationship. You can only do your best and provide the most skillful guidance possible. Your client must choose whether or not to be open and use the knowledge you offer.

Imagine yourself as a medical doctor who has diagnosed a patient with diabetes. You can prescribe medication and lifestyle modifications, but you can't force the patient to take pills on a daily basis, test his blood regularly, and change his eating habits. The ultimate success of the treatment is up to him.

In counseling, you give "emotional medication" rather than pills. You guide a client to changes that will result in good emotional health. But just as a doctor can't force a patient to comply with a treatment protocol, you can't force your client to implement the changes. If he refuses to participate in the treatment plan, you can't allow yourself to feel responsible for the outcome as long as you've made your best effort.

CLIENT CHALLENGES

As described previously, many of the difficulties you'll face as a counselor are based on your interactions with clients. These can range from a fairly mild issue, such as trying to draw someone into participating when they have no motivation, to a serious situation in which you're dealing with a suicidal client. Let's look at a few of these client-based challenges in more depth:

Reluctant/Unmotivated Clients

Virtually every counselor will encounter reluctant or unmotivated clients at some point in her career. If you work in certain environments, this issue is more common. For example, you might work in a government-funded program and facilitate a parenting group for mothers and fathers who've had their children removed by the court. Some participants may be angry and resentful because they're being forced to attend. If you work at a substance abuse clinic or do anger management therapy, you might have court-ordered clients who have been arrested for driving while intoxicated or abusing their spouse. These clients may be defensive and blind to the need for treatment. They'll continue with the sessions because it keeps them out of jail, but they won't internalize anything you try to teach them.

Even if you're in private or group practice, working with clients who voluntarily seek out counseling, you'll discover that some will drop out as soon as they realize you can't magically solve all their problems. Many people don't understand exactly how counseling works. They expect a counselor to give them direct advice and solutions rather than guiding them to their own insights. Some may have a victim mentality and want their counselor to agree and sympathize. What they really need is to gain understanding of why that viewpoint is unhealthy and how they can escape from it. Some may want to vent and complain, but they'll get disgruntled when

As a counselor, you must be prepared to depersonalize from the parts of your job over which you have no control.

the counselor tries to help them see how they can change the situation.

When you encounter these challenges, redirect your focus to the bigger picture. Even if you cannot help every client, you'll make a life changing difference for those who are willing to do the work. Not everyone who stops in a clothing store will end up buying a new outfit. Not everyone who enters your office will continue to come or participate actively, but when they do their reward will be far beyond a new suit or dress.

Personal Insight

FROM THE AUTHOR: I like to address the issue of motivation right from the start with my clients. I make it into a joke, saying, "I thought I'd get a magic wand with my diploma, but no such luck. I'd love to be able to tap you on the head and remove all your problems, but in reality it's going to take a lot of work. I can't promise fast and easy solutions, but I can promise that the end result will be worth it if you're willing to stick with this."

Most people respond well to humor, and at the same time I've let them know what to expect. Down the road, if they ever press for a quick fix, I can remind them, "I warned you before that I don't have a magic wand. I know it's frustrating to work through things slowly, but that's the only way to find a permanent solution." Usually that's all it takes to redirect them.

Suicidal Clients

One of the most frightening prospects for a counselor is the risk of working with a suicidal client who follows through successfully. This is a very real possibility. One study found that out of 376 professional counselors, nearly 24 percent had a client in their primary care who committed suicide (McAdams & Foster, 2000). This event has a significant, lasting impact on a counselor's personal and professional life. It can bring out feelings of sadness, anger, and even guilt (McAdams & Foster, 2002).

You can put safeguards into place, but when a client is living on his own with no solid reason for hospitalization, there's no way you can be 100 percent certain that he won't make a suicide attempt. This is true even if he makes verbal promises, agrees to a written plan, and signs a suicide contract.

Because every person is unique and so many factors play into each individual case, there is no foolproof way to assess a client's suicide risk. However, you can look at some general factors such as these:

- Has the client's suicidal ideation started recently, or is it an old idea?

> *You can put safeguards into place, but when a client is living on his own with no solid reason for hospitalization, there's no way you can be 100 percent certain that he won't make a suicide attempt.*

- Has the client ever made a suicide attempt previously?
- Does the client have a specific suicide plan that includes the method by which he will do it and a timeframe to carry it out?
- Does the client have the means and opportunity to realistically carry out his plan?
- Does the client have a strong support network he can turn to if he is feeling desperate, and is he willing to reach out to them?
- Is the client exhibiting severe depressive symptoms that are interfering with his functioning?
- Is the client facing severe stressors, such as divorce, job loss, a home foreclosure, serious illness, or the death of a loved one?
- Does the client have emotional issues that could play into the situation, such as severe guilt feelings or dangerously low self esteem?
- What is the client's usual coping pattern for severe stress?

If you suspect that someone may be in danger of attempting suicide but aren't sure whether he meets the legal criteria for mandated reporting, talk to your supervisor or ask for guidance from a trusted peer.

If your client does harm or kill himself despite your best efforts, it's essential to turn to your personal and professional support systems. Research shows that support from an immediate supervisor, as well family and friends can play a critical role in recovering from the trauma (McAdams & Foster, 2002).

In addition to working through your own emotions, you might face a legal battle. Family members will sometimes file a lawsuit, even if there are no legitimate grounds, in an effort to find somewhere to place the blame and get a financial settlement. Suicide is devastating to those left behind, and they often grasp at any way to make sense of what happened. If you have insurance, you'll be financially protected but you'll still face an emotional toll.

If you tend to be a sensitive person, be aware of the fact that you might have to make peace with losing a client in this manner someday. If you don't think you would be able to do that, or you don't want to take responsibility for suicidal clients, counseling may not be the best career. Consider an option such as life coaching where you can do similar work, but with clients whose issues are unlikely to end in suicide. Alternately, you can choose an area of practice where the chances of encountering a suicidal client are minimal, such as vocational counseling.

MANDATED REPORTING

As a mental health professional, you will be mandated by law to break confidentiality and report clients in certain circumstances. This is often referred to as the "duty to warn" and the "duty to protect." In general, reporting is required when a client is seriously planning to harm himself or someone else. Clients who reveal that they are abusing a child or elderly family member can also fall under the mandated reporting laws. When you encounter these situations, you have no choice but to report them to the proper authorities or you could face legal consequences.

Reporting Danger to a Person or Property

The precedent for this requirement was set by a 1976 California case, Tarasoff v. Regents of the University of California. It involved a counselor who didn't warn a young woman and her parents when specific death threats were made against them by a client. The woman was subsequently killed, and her family sued the counselor for failing to warn her of the potential danger. More recent court cases have expanded on the Tasaroff ruling, and states have their own laws, but the main guideline seems to be "counselor/client privilege ends where the public peril begins."

Unfortunately, choosing to warn can also open a counselor up to liability if the client decides to sue. While some states offer protection, in others the client doesn't have to be in the right legally in order to file a lawsuit if he feels that you wrongly breached his confidentiality. You must be prepared to prove that you had a strong reason to believe someone was in danger and that it was enough to justify your choice of action.

It's a tricky situation, but there are three basic principles to help you assess your potential liability:

- **Is there clearly foreseeable harm?** For example, has the client made a verbal threat to a potential victim? Is the threat believable? A counselor must judge this by deciding whether the threat is specific and doable or whether it is too vague or exaggerated to be taken seriously. In making this decision, the counselor also should consider whether the client has an ongoing history of making threats and acting out violently and if he has a motive.

- **Can the victim be identified and/or has the client mentioned specific property he plans to damage?** The victim may be a third party, or it can be the client himself if he is threatening suicide, self mutilation or other personal harm. If he directs the threat at an unidentified person or a general group or category, you cannot carry out a duty to warn because you don't know exactly who or what is in danger.

- **Is it feasible for the counselor to intervene?** What would that intervention be? Would you call the authorities, notify the endangered person yourself, or both? Know your state's laws in regard to how notifications must be handled and follow them exactly. If you have any questions, consult an attorney who is familiar with the laws governing mental health practice.

As an example, let's say that you have a client who is bitter over his divorce. During your counseling sessions, he might make comments like, "We would never have split if it wasn't for my ex-wife's family. They were always meddling and making trouble telling her how bad I was. I'd love to get back at her mother for screwing up our relationship."

Is this a circumstance that needs to be reported? The client has identified a potential victim, and his words could be taken as a threat. However, in this case it's rather vague. He could mean that he'd like to get back at his ex-mother-in-law by burning down her house, but he could also mean that he'd simply like to tell her off. In this case, there is no clearly foreseeable harm, so it wouldn't fit under the mandatory reporting requirements.

If your client said, "I'm going to get back at my mother-in-law for breaking us up. She'd better watch out because one day very soon her tires are going to be slashed and her car is going to be keyed," that would be a different matter. These threats are much more specific and involve specific acts against a particular person and a clearly defined piece of property. If you truly believe that your client means to carry out this threat, you might need to warn his mother-in-law or notify the proper authorities.

In addition to state law, some counselors may fall under the requirements of the Health Insurance Portability and Accountability Act (HIPAA), which dictates certain privacy rules. This depends on where they work and in what capacity. Protect yourself by staying up to date on your state's laws and knowing if HIPAA is applicable. If it is, your employer will probably have an official policy in place. Strict compliance with legal requirements will help protect you from potential liability if someone files suit because you broke their confidence.

Reporting Child and/or Elder Abuse

Under the Federal Child Abuse Prevention and Treatment Act (CAPTA), which was passed in 1974, all 50 states have implemented some type of law mandating the reporting of child abuse and neglect. However, the specific laws can vary widely from state to state. Some cover school counselors, while others require reporting by any professional counselor. Know the laws in your area of practice and specific locale, especially if you work with youngsters frequently.

For example, perhaps you're conducting family therapy with a couple and their two sons. Several times you've noticed suspicious bruises on one or both of the boys. When you ask about it, the boys look embarrassed and refuse to talk. Their parents always have an explanation like, "Oh, he fell off his skateboard" or "He tripped and bumped the coffee table." Because you are seeing concrete evidence of injury and the stories are not adding up, you may be required to report this situation as potential child abuse case.

Depending on the state, professional counselors may also be required to report cases of elder abuse and neglect. Reportable circumstances usually include physical, emotional or sexual abuse; passive neglect or willful deprivation; confinement; and financial exploitation.

For example, you might be counseling a teenage girl who tells you that her mother has struck her elderly grandfather. The grandfather lives with the family and is physically disabled and confined to his bed, so he requires a great deal of care. Your client confides that her mother gets very frustrated when attending to his needs. If he moves around too much when she is trying to dress him or change his sheets, she sometimes slaps or punches him. Your client has even noticed bruises on her grandfather after some of these incidents. Because it's likely that a helpless elderly person is being harmed, this circumstance might fall under your state's mandated reporting laws.

Personal Safety

Because mental health counselors work with clients who are dealing with emotional issues, and are typically in a one-on-one situation, there is always a risk of violence. The Occupational Health and Safety Administration (OSHA) says that the social service and health care industries face the highest risk of assault of any private industry. Students and interns are in the greatest danger, with 46% of assaults involving these populations. Fortunately, incidents of violence steadily decrease as a counselor's experience level rises

Even when an attack doesn't result in serious physical injury, it can have wide-ranging emotional effects for the victim. Some of these include a loss of confidence in their ability to continue to work effectively, anger, guilt, self-blame, guilt, anger about the episode, and ongoing safety concerns (Littlechild, 1995).

Degree programs in counseling rarely address how to evaluate the risk of violence with aggressive clients and how to defuse a potentially volatile situation. One study revealed that less than a quarter of the participants had received any training in this area while in school (Moscovitch, Chaimowitz & Patterson, 1990). This means that when confronted with a potentially dangerous situation, most counselors have no preparation for how to handle it.

There are several ways in which counselors can take responsibility for their own protection. These include:

- **Carefully screening your clients.** Know which people might have an increased risk of acting out or exhibiting violent behavior. This will allow you to be extra vigilant when needed, rec-

Degree programs in counseling rarely address how to evaluate the risk of violence with aggressive clients and how to defuse a potentially volatile situation.

ognize signs early and put a halt to the situation before it escalates.

- ***Keeping potential weapons put away.*** Innocent items such as scissors, paperweights, and letter openers can turn into dangerous weapons if they get into the hands of a violent person. Keep your desk and other surfaces free of any articles that could be used against you in a volatile situation.

- ***Making an excuse to get out of the situation before it escalates.*** If you sense that a client may be getting worked up and moving towards a violent outburst, try to diffuse the situation by finding a reason to leave the room. Say you need to get some water, use the restroom, or any other non-threatening excuse that would give you a reason to physically remove yourself.

- ***Positioning yourself to have an easy exit.*** Arrange your office furniture so that your chair is positioned with a direct line to the door. If a client tries to physically attack you, this will increase your chances of getting out, alerting others, and running to safety.

- ***Never working alone.*** The mental health professional often involves working flexible hours, which may include evenings and weekends. Even though the office might be quieter than usual during those times, there should always be at least one other person present.

- ***Learning how to defend yourself.*** Taking a course in self-defense techniques can be invaluable. Although you might not be able to overpower a physically violent client, you can learn how to dodge him, break his hold, and get out of the office. You can also keep a small canister of pepper spray within easy reach to disable a client while you escape.

DEALING WITH INSURANCE COMPANIES

Many insurance plans offer mental health benefits for therapy sessions with a licensed professional counselor. If you are willing to bill insurance companies directly, or you work for an office that does, it will greatly expand your potential client base. It has its downside, too, as you will almost certainly face paperwork challenges, treatment limitations, and payment delays and denials.

Paperwork

If you are working in a position that requires you to deal with insurance companies in order to get reimbursement for your services, you may find yourself buried in a nightmare mountain of paperwork. Because of this, many counselors in private practice outsource their billing or only work with clients who are paying out of pocket.

Working with self-pays eliminates the problem, but it also limits the client base since many people cannot afford to pay the entire cost of regular therapy sessions out of pocket. To offset this, some counselors charge lower rates if they don't accept insurance. They can afford to do this because they don't have the overhead of paying someone to do the billing. This allows clients to more easily afford to self-pay.

Treatment Limitations

If you work in a group practice or agency where someone else handles the insurance claims, you may still face frustration caused by the limits imposed by managed care plans. For example, you might feel that a proper treatment plan would take twelve weeks, but the client's insurance company will only approve eight sessions. If the client cannot afford to pay for the additional sessions out of pocket, you will have to adapt the schedule to fit within the insurance company's requirements. This requires both flexibility and creativity on the counselor's part. Taking classes or seminars in brief therapy techniques may help.

Personal Insight

Mary Robbins, LCSW, a social worker practicing in Connecticut, has faced her share of challenges when dealing with insurance companies. She cites the time she loses to dealing with insurance issues as one of her biggest professional frustrations.

"The insurance companies pay a significantly lower dollar amount then a practitioner receives from private pay clients, so right off the bat you are at a loss," she explains.

"The insurance companies require a lot of paperwork from clinicians--billing paperwork using their coding, treatment plans using their individual forms, and just the initial paperwork to be registered or paneled on the boards. I hired another person to complete all of it for each company; most of us do (hire someone) to get through the maze.

"If you don't comply by submitting a treatment plan in time and you have already met with the client, you can't expect to be paid for that time. They are really trying to limit the amount of sessions offered to the client; their sole purpose is to balance saving money and treatment, and they are somewhat 'brainwashed' that only brief treatment works.

"Most private practice clinicians are the only people doing the enormous amounts of paperwork, record keeping, treatment plans, submission of invoices and tracking of sessions and tracking if the session was paid by the insurance company, unlike a physician who can afford to hire an entire staff. If insurance isn't used, the therapist writes a treatment note, the client pays them and the transaction takes all of 10 to 15 minutes. Using insurance, it can take an hour per client."

The length of time it takes to receive a payment can also cause hardships. Mary says insurers can take a month or longer to pay for the services. "And if there is a dispute, that check can take forever!" she exclaims. "I wish I could tell the gas company, 'but the insurance company hasn't paid me yet and won't for a month, so don't shut off the gas.'"

PROFESSIONAL LIABILITY

Whenever you work with clients in a care giver/care receiver relationship, you expose yourself to potential lawsuits. Even if you're always careful and adhere strictly to professional ethics and legal restrictions, you could still face a suit from a disgruntled client. While the suit may not be successful, you'll still have to go through the time and trouble of defending it and possibly suffer a loss of reputation no matter what the outcome turns out to be.

In a 1999 survey of licensed psychologists, almost 40 percent reported knowing a colleague who had been sued for malpractice, and 7.4 percent of respondents said they had personally been threatened with a lawsuit. Of those who received a threat, 57.1 percent said that the client followed through and filed a suit (Montgomery, Cupit, & Wimberley, 1999).

Protecting Yourself

How can you protect yourself from lawsuits? While there's no way to shield yourself completely, knowing the law and taking care to fulfill your legal and ethical responsibilities will put you in the best position possible.

Counselors should always carry a professional liability insurance policy. If you work for a business or government agency, they will most likely have a policy that covers you. Ask your supervisor to be sure. If you're in private practice or work as an independent contractor in a group practice, you'll be responsible for finding your own coverage. Many professional organizations, such as the American Counseling Association, offer discounted policies to their members.

If you are in private practice, you may also wish to consider forming a corporation or a limited liability company (LLC) as a way to shield your personal assets. If you conduct business through a corporation or LLC, those personal assets may be protected in case of a lawsuit because it's actually the business entity being sued. None of this should be taken as legal advice. Consult an attorney to discuss the potential benefits and drawbacks, including the level of protection that might be offered and whether it's worth the cost and paperwork involved.

In a 1999 survey of licensed psychologists, almost 40 percent reported knowing a colleague who had been sued for malpractice, and 7.4 percent of respondents said they had personally been threatened with a lawsuit.

PERSONAL CHALLENGES

Being a professional counselor can take a toll on your personal life once you leave the office. When you spend your workday listening to problems, issues, and challenges, it can be quite draining. It's easy to let yourself get drawn in a little too far. A good counselor has empathy, but it's a fine line between maintaining a caring sense of detachment and crossing over to personal involvement. If you do, you'll quickly be emotionally tapped, and this will spill over onto dealing with your family and friends. You have to be prepared to maintain solid boundaries to protect yourself. You should rely on your professional support network to sort through work-related issues and put them aside when you walk out the office door.

Personal Insight

Sue Carberry, a counselor in the United Kingdom, agrees that remembering not to take the clients' issues home with her is one of the most challenging parts of her work. She credits her peers and supervisors with helping her to avoid this trap: "I have regular supervision and work with some brilliant people to keep me balanced, healthy and centered."

Mary Robbins, LCSW, a licensed social worker practicing in Connecticut, brings up another area in which working in the mental health field can affect your personal life. She says, "Telling people what you do is an immediate turn off. They often stop talking to you thinking you are analyzing them." This gives yet another reason to maintain that personal/professional separation.

CHAPTER SUMMARY

- There are a number of professional challenges that are common to counseling work.
- Client-based challenges include working with reluctant or unmotivated clients or having someone commit suicide while under your treatment.
- Counselors must know their responsibilities under mandated reporting laws, which require them to break confidentiality in certain circumstances where a client poses a danger to himself and/or others.
- Even though they may not receive training on how to deal with potentially violent clients, counselors should take their own safety precautions.
- Insurance companies can cause frustration due to excessive paperwork and treatment limitations.
- Counselors should maintain professional liability insurance due to the risk of being sued.
- Incorporating or forming a limited liability company may help counselors protect their personal assets.

PART TWO

The Nuts and Bolts
of Becoming a Counselor

YOUR EDUCATION

You've considered the traits that make a good counselor and they read like a description of your own personality. You like the idea of helping others, the future prospect for jobs look good, and you think you can live with the salary. You're willing to make the educational and financial commitments. What now?

EARNING YOUR DEGREE

The first step in becoming a counselor is to get your college education. The licensure requirements in virtually every state require a counselor to have a master's degree from an accredited school. This degree may be either an **M. A.** (Master of Arts) or an **M. S.** (Master of Science) in counseling, psychology or a closely related subject, but the requirements will be similar at all accredited schools.

IF YOU'RE CURRENTLY IN HIGH SCHOOL

According to the U. S. Department of Education National Center for Education, in 2005 69 percent of high school graduates enrolled in college in the fall semester immediately following their completion date. If you're currently a high school student who is planning to become a counselor, you're probably going to join them.

Some graduates take a break before starting college for a variety of reasons. These typically include taking a temporary breather from academics; doing more research and preparation before choosing a college; exploring career choices in more depth before committing to a major; or working for a year or two to earn money for tuition.

If you are confident in your choice of a becoming a professional counselor, you can do a lot of preparation during high school to prepare you for a smooth transition directly into college. By not taking a break, you avoid the risk of losing motivation or getting sidetracked by unexpected circumstances.

Your First Step

Your ultimate academic goal is to earn a master's degree in counseling. The first step in this process is to gain admission to an undergraduate program and earn a Bachelors degree, preferably in psychology or a closely related field. There are many ways to prepare for this step throughout your high school years. These include:

- *Earning high grades.* Maintaining a high grade point average through all four years of high school will help you get into the undergraduate program of your choice. It may also qualify you for scholarship opportunities. Even though you can recover if your grades slip early on, it will look better on your college admission applications if you have a consistently excellent performance. If you have a high enough grade point average, you may qualify for the National Honor Society, which will also look good on applications.
- *Taking appropriate classes.* If your school offers psychology and social science-related classes, sign up for as many as you can. This will give you a head start on learning the fundamentals. These subjects are the foundation of your higher education and your eventual career.
- *Participating in your school's psychology club if it has one.* Many schools have clubs related to various subjects or career interests. If your school doesn't already have a psychology club, you may be able to start one. For more information on how to do this, provided by the American Psychological Association, visit www.apa.org/ed/topss/psych_club.html. You will need to enlist the aid of your psychology teacher.
- *Participating in other extracurricular activities.* Being active in high school will look good on your college applications. Participating in clubs and activities may also help you qualify for related scholarships. Aim for a good mix of service, academic and social clubs to present a well-rounded picture.
- *Taking advanced placement(AP) classes.* Some high schools offer classes that allow you to earn college credit during your senior year. Subjects include psychology, biology, physics, statistics, literature, art history, music theory and more. If your school has this program, be sure to take advantage of it to get a jump-start on college. Getting credit

If you are confident in your choice of a becoming a professional counselor, you can do a lot of preparation during high school to prepare you for a smooth transition directly into college.

for general education subjects frees you to take more electives of interest.

- ***Taking part in career preparation programs.*** Many high schools have career days or job fairs, where professionals working in various fields visit your school and talk to interested students. If your school offers this opportunity, be sure to participate if there is a speaker representing the counseling field. You'll hear firsthand about what it takes to become a professional counselor, how you would spend a typical day, and the pros and cons of the job. Usually you'll also have the opportunity to ask the speaker questions and perhaps even meet with her for a one-on-one discussion.

- ***Talking to your school counselor about your interest in a counseling career.*** As professionals in the field, school counselors can give you a firsthand perspective and information based on their own personal experience. They'll guide you through the often confusing path of preparing for your undergraduate and graduate degrees and what to look for in a college. They may even be willing to share some personal insights based on their own journey to the field.

- ***Volunteering at a social service agency or other provider of counseling services.*** Even if you can only spare an hour or two each week, you'll get a flavor for this type of work and whether it would make an appealing career. If your high school has a community service requirement, this volunteer work might fulfill it. Even if you don't have to earn community service credit, gaining hands-on experience in a social service environment will give you a small taste of what your future workplace might be like.

Junior Year

Once you reach your junior year, preparation for college will begin in earnest. Here are some of the tasks on which you'll need to focus:

- ***Starting your college search.*** Locate suitable schools and request information about their programs and admission requirements. Collegeboard.com provides an online tool where you can keep a personal list of schools of interest. You can access it at www.collegeboard.com/ student/apply/the-application/568.html. If you live near a major metropolitan area, you may also want to visit a college fair. You can find more information about national college fairs at www.nacacnet.org/ eventstraining/collegefairs/Pages/default.aspx

    Always make sure that the schools you are considering are accredited by the appropriate agency. You'll find more information on accreditation later in this chapter.

- ***Estimating your costs and start your financial aid search.*** You can use the college cost estimator at www.collegeboard.com/student/

pay/add-it-up/401.html and the scholarship search tool at http://apps. collegeboard.com/cbsearch_ss/welcome.jsp.

- ***Taking the Preliminary SAT/National Merit Scholarship Qualifying Test.*** This exam is co-sponsored program by the College Board and National Merit Scholarship Corporation (NMSC), and it helps prepare you to take the SAT test in your senior year. It can also qualify you for NMSC scholarships. Areas covered include critical reading skills, math problem-solving, and writing. You can find practice questions at www.collegeboard.com/student/testing/psat/prep.html.
- ***Taking the SAT and/or ACT test.*** While the SAT is the more popular of the two, some schools may have a preference for the ACT. The SAT covers reading, writing, and math while the ACT covers these same subjects and also science.

Senior Year

When you reach your last year of high school, you'll be in the final stages of preparation. Although there will be some other items, much of your task list will be focused on applying to colleges and making decisions based on the responses you receive. Here are the main tasks:

- Take any advanced placement (AP) tests and College-Level Examination Program (CLEP) exams for which you might qualify. You can find more information on CLEP in Chapter Seven.
- Narrow down your college list and send out your applications.
- Submit an application for financial aid. You can find the Free Application for Federal Student Aid at www.fafsa.ed.gov. You will need your parents' income tax figures in order to apply so they should fill out their forms as soon as possible after January 1 in your senior year.
- Sort through your acceptances, make your choice, and send in your tuition down payment.
- Gear up for the next leg of your journey to a counseling career. You can find more in-depth information on how to prepare for college throughout your high school years on the National Association for College Admission Counseling (NACAC) website at www.nacacnet.org/StudentResources/CollegePrep/Pages/default.aspx.

Homeschoolers

According to the U. S. Department of Education, as of 2007 there were 1.1 million students who were being home schooled in the United States. While these students might be high performers, they don't have official transcripts and records like their counterparts in public and private schools. This can put up some barriers to the college application process.

Fortunately more colleges are recognizing the needs of this growing population and taking steps to accommodate it. According to the NACAC, in 2000 only 52 percent of colleges had a formal evaluation process in place for homeschooled applicants. By 2004, that number had jumped to 83 percent. If this trend continues, homeschoolers will soon be on equal footing with those who attend public and private schools.

What If You're Not Accepted?

Even if you put forth your best effort, you might not be accepted by any of the schools to which you have submitted applications. This is rare, but it can happen if you choose highly competitive schools or if you made some bad decisions in high school that affected your applications negatively. For example, if you earned bad grades early on, they might pull your grade point average down even if you recovered in the latter part of your high school years.

If this happens, you have two options: choose an alternate school with lower admissions standards, or attend a community college for the first two years. Then you can transfer to your preferred school to complete the last two years of your Bachelors degree. If you earn top grades at a community college, it will boost your chances of being admitted to your school of choice as a transfer student.

IF YOU'RE CURRENTLY IN COLLEGE

If you're currently enrolled in an undergraduate program, you should start your search for a graduate program as soon as possible and prepare to send out your applications. This process typically includes the following:

* ***Maintain a high grade point average in your undergraduate coursework.*** You should aim for at least 3.0 or higher on a 4.0 grade scale, as this is the minimum requirement for many graduate programs.
* ***Complete appropriate prerequisite courses.*** For a degree in counseling psychology, these might include: Introduction to Psychology, Biological Psychology, Research Methods, Abnormal Psychology and Statistics for the Social Sciences. You may also be required to have taken a certain number of courses or semester hours in psychology or behavioral science courses.
* ***Complete a test such as the Graduate Record Examinations (GRE).*** The GRE is a commercially run standardized test that is used by many U.S. colleges and universities for admission to their graduate programs. There is a general GRE that measures a student's verbal reasoning ability, quantitative reasoning, critical thinking, and analytical writing skills. There are also several tests on specific subjects, including one for psychology.

The psychology test is made up of multiple choice questions that cover material typically learned in a quality undergraduate program. A high score shows prospective schools that you've got the necessary foundation to embark on graduate studies. You can download a test booklet for the GRE in psychology to get an idea of what it covers from www.ets.org/Media/Tests/GRE/pdf/Psychology.pdf.

- ***Prepare a list of personal, work and/or academic references.*** These should be people who can attest to your good character, academic ability, and potential for success in graduate school. They may need to provide a letter of recommendation, or the schools to which you apply may have their own forms.
- ***Prepare an admittance essay or statement of purpose.*** Some of the typical things that schools will ask you to include are a statement of your goals, your reasons for pursuing a graduate degree, your plans for a professional career, and an honest assessment of your strengths and weaknesses.
- ***Fill out your applications and submit them.*** An application usually requires basic information about yourself, your family background, your previous academic history, any clubs, associations and organizations you might belong to, honors and awards you have received, community service work you've done, and a personal statement that describes your future goals and ambitions. Most schools will require you to pay a non-refundable fee along with the application.

  If you are not a native speaker of the English language, you may also be required to submit TOEFL scores. TOEFL is the Test of English as a Foreign Language, and it measures your ability and fluency to ensure that you have the appropriate language skills to be able to go through a graduate program.
- ***Be prepared to be called in for interviews.*** If they are seriously considering your application, most schools will set up an interview to get to know you better. Typically you'll meet with faculty members, department heads, and other officials within the school's admissions and psychology departments.

CHOOSING THE RIGHT SCHOOL

The quality of your education and training is directly tied to the quality of the university you attend and its specific counseling program.

Your choice of school will lay the foundation for your counseling career. The quality of your education and training is directly tied to the quality of the university you attend and its specific counseling program. Fortunately you won't have to choose a school blindly. By selecting an accredited school and program you'll know that it's already been screened and that you have a reasonable assurance of a high-quality education. It's important to know the difference between school and program accreditation because you'll need to look for both when evaluating potential graduate schools.

ACCREDITED SCHOOLS

As you hunt for a college, you may hear a lot of talk about "accreditation." Prospective students should always choose an accredited school, whether they plan to attend college at a bricks and mortar location or to earn a degree online, to ensure that their degree will be recognized by future employers and licensing boards.

What is School Accreditation?

At its most basic, when a school is it has passed a quality review conducted by an accrediting agency. Its policies and programs are scrutinized by the agency to see if they meet the set criteria. If they do, the school receives its accreditation. Colleges that are not accredited might offer substandard classes that won't properly prepare you for a professional career. By checking for accreditation, you'll avoid falling prey to these questionable schools.

It's not difficult to find an accredited school, as there are literally thousands throughout the United States. As of October, 2008, the Council for Higher Education Accreditation (CHEA) reported that there were almost 4500 accredited degree-granting colleges and universities throughout the country.

School Accreditation Agencies

Accreditation is only as good as the agency that is providing it. There are six regional accreditation agencies that are recognized by the United States Department of Education (USDE) and the Council for Higher Education Accreditation (CHEA), which means they are legitimate. Each of these agencies handles schools in multiple states. They are:

The New England Association of Schools and Colleges (NEASC), which accredits schools in Connecticut, Maine, Massachusetts, New Hampshire, Rhode Island, and Vermont. Their website is www.neasc.org.

The North Central Association Commission on Accreditation and School Improvement (NCA), which accredits schools in Arizona, Arkansas, Colorado, Illinois, Indiana, Iowa, Kansas, Michigan, Minnesota, Missouri, Navajo Nation, Nebraska, New Mexico, North Dakota, Ohio, Oklahoma, South Dakota, West Virginia, Wis-

Colleges that are not accredited might offer substandard classes that won't properly prepare you for a professional career.

consin, and Wyoming. Their website is www.ncacasi.org.

The Middle States Association of Schools and Colleges (MSA), which accredits schools in Delaware, the District of Columbia, Maryland, New Jersey, New York, and Pennsylvania. Their website is www.middlestates.org.

The Southern Association of Schools and Colleges (SACS), which accredits schools in Alabama, Florida, Georgia, Kentucky, Louisiana, Mississippi, North Carolina, South Carolina, Tennessee, Texas and Virginia. Their website is www.sacs.org.

The Western Association of Schools and Colleges (WASC), which accredits schools in California and Hawaii. Their website is www.wascweb.org.

The Northwest Association of Schools and Colleges (NWCCU), which accredits schools in Alaska, Idaho, Montana, Nevada, Oregon, Utah, and Washington State. Their website is www.nwccu.org.

Always make sure that the colleges you are considering are accredited by one of these agencies. If you have any questions about a school's status, contact the appropriate agency to verify that it is currently accredited.

ACCREDITED PROGRAMS

Accreditation of a program is different than accreditation of a school, although it serves the same basic purpose of assuring a certain level of quality. Once you have determined that the colleges you are considering have legitimate accreditation, you should narrow down the list by checking to see if their actual counseling program is accredited.

Who Accredits Counseling Programs?

The Council for Accreditation of Counseling and Related Educational Programs (CACREP) is the recognized accreditation agency for graduate counseling programs. Accreditation means that a counseling program meets the standards laid out by the accreditation agency. By choosing a school with a CACREP-accredited program you have some assurance that your education will meet state licensing requirements. If you know where you will be practicing when you are done with your program, check that state's specific requirements to confirm that it will.

CACREP Requirements

CACREP's standards as of July, 2009, can be found on their website at www.cacrep.org/2009standards.html. Some of the highlights include requiring all students to have a faculty advisor throughout the program; a ratio of full-time students to faculty that does not exceed 10 to 1; ongoing assessment of the students' academic, personal and professional progress; and assessment of students' adherence to the American Counseling Association (ACA) code of ethics.

CACREP also spells out the knowledge and skills required by the most common counseling specialties: addictions counseling; career counseling; mental health counseling; marriage, couple and family counseling; and school counseling for grade school, high school and college. The required core curriculum includes classes in: Professional Identity, Social and Cultural Diversity, Human Growth and Development; Career Development; Helping Relationships; Group Work; Assessment; and Research and Program Evaluation.

CACREP standards lay out guidelines for the practicum and internship. Students in an accredited program are required to complete a supervised practicum of 100 clock hours over the course of a 10-week semester. At least 40 hours of the practicum must be spent in direct service delivery with clients. After the practicum, a 600 hour internship must be completed, with 240 of those hours being spent in direct service delivery doing individual or group work with clients.

CACREP accredits both traditional and online schools. To find out whether a program you are considering is CACREP accredited, visit the directory on their website which can be found at www.cacrep.org/directory.html.

TYPICAL CLASSES

Even CACREP-accredited counseling programs will have some variance, depending on the school and your area of specialization. For example, if you're studying to be a substance abuse counselor, many of your classes will be geared towards addiction theory and treatment. If you want to be a school counselor, the bulk of your courses will focus on dealing with youngsters and their social and education-related issues, as well as recognizing and dealing with emotional and learning disabilities.

Because mental health counselors deal with a wide cross-section of clients, their typical curriculum offers a good overview of the types of classes you'll be required to take. The classes and descriptions below represent a very general sample of graduate level courses for aspiring mental health counselors. The names and description vary by school, but your program should be similar:

Theories of Personality: As the name implies, this course will provide you with an overview of various personality theories. You will learn how to apply this knowledge when you interact with clients in a professional counseling situation.

Counseling Foundations: This course lays out the basic concepts for conducting therapy sessions with adults, children, couples and families. It will help you develop core counseling skills. You'll begin to develop your professional identity, and you'll also learn how to build a strong therapeutic relationship with your clients.

Human Growth and Development: This course explores all facets of human development. It covers birth, childhood, adolescence, adulthood, and old age. You'll learn about individual and family development and examine the ways in which various life cycle issues affect human relationships.

Social and Cultural Foundations: In this course, you'll develop an understanding of the cultural and ethnic attributes of potential clients and the ways in which they might affect the counseling relationship. You'll examine such concepts as gender roles, ethnic groups, subcultures, urban and rural societies, and cultural mores. You'll also learn about the role of counseling professionals in confronting and eliminating biases and oppression in society as a whole and on an individual basis.

Psychopathology: In this course, you'll examine major psychological disorders as described in the current Diagnostic and Statistic Manual of Mental Disorders. You'll gain familiarity with how these disorders manifest themselves and learn to recognize their typical symptoms. You'll also learn about the treatment and management of affected clients.

Psychopharmacology: This course will introduce you to typical pharmacological agents that affect mental and emotional functions. You'll learn about common psychotropic drugs that are used to treat psychopathological disorders. You'll also look at factors such as their typical rate of effectiveness in treating a disorder and their potential side effects. This class will teach you about medications that can potentially be abused and how you can recognize signs that this might be happening with a client.

Psychological Assessment: This course examines various methods used by counselors for assessing the functioning of individuals, groups, and families. You'll learn about commonly used tests such as the Minnesota Multiphasic Personality Inventory (MMPI), intelligence tests such as the Wechsler Adult Intelligence Scale (WAIS), and projective tests like the Thematic Appreciation Test (TAT). You'll also learn how to administer and score these tests, how to gather and interpret data, and how to broaden your interpretations to a multicultural perspective.

Psychodiagnostics: This course will teach you to develop diagnostic and treatment strategies that can be used in clinical practice. You'll learn how to choose an appropriate therapeutic model for a particular case, and you'll be able recognize the indications/contraindications for various kinds of therapy. You'll gain the skills necessary to apply this information to your client's specific situation and create an appropriate treatment plan.

Human Sexuality: In this course, you'll examine the various theories surrounding human sexuality. You'll also look at the physiological, psychological, and sociocultural variables associated with sexual identity, behaviors, and sex-related disorders.

Counseling Techniques: This course will teach you how to develop an effective helping relationship with your clients. You'll have the opportunity to practice basic communications skills that strengthen the therapeutic alliance. You'll also learn to help clients identify their issues and create specific goals for counseling. You'll participate in role play situations that allow you to try out your new skills in a controlled environment.

Group Counseling Techniques: This course will prepare you to facilitate group therapy sessions. You'll explore group theory and discuss the various types of therapy groups and their dynamics. You'll also learn about appropriate treatment methods and develop the necessary skills for successful group facilitation. You'll also learn special strategies for working with groups effectively in a multicultural society.

Substance Abuse Counseling: This course will give you an overview of the typical behavior patterns of drug and alcohol users and teach you about the methods used to treat them. Depending on the scope, you may also cover other types of addictions, including gambling, shopping, spending, pornography and sex, and eating disorders such as anorexia and bulimia.

Research and Evaluation: In this course, you will focus on statistics and the research design process. You'll learn how to develop research and demonstration proposals and how to interpret the results. You'll also discuss the relevance and importance of research in the field of counseling and what can be gained by conducting well-designed studies, both in a controlled setting and out in the real world.

Electives: In addition to these mandatory courses, you will be allowed to self-select from a variety of classes to round out your credit hour requirements. While all of these courses are generally related to psychology and/or the field of counseling, they can vary widely in their specific subject matter. Some might be advanced levels of the required courses, while others might cover a counseling specialty or working with a sub-set of the population. Often there will be a course focused on the latest trends and research.

While this varies widely by school, topics may include Crisis Intervention, Industrial Psychology, Advanced Personality Theory, Advanced Psychobiology, Career Development, Working With Special Needs Students, Current Issues and Trends in Psychology, or Brief Therapy Techniques.

Choosing Your Electives

When choosing electives, consider the following questions to help you make the best choices:

- *Which therapeutic techniques would you like to learn more about?* If you have an affinity for a certain technique, electives can give you the opportunity to study it in more depth. You may be able to take advanced classes that will teach you how to apply it in hands-on settings.

If you're curious about an unfamiliar type of therapy, you can choose a related elective to learn what it's all about and whether it might be useful for you.

- **Which population would you like to work with as a professional counselor?** Many schools offer electives covering special populations. These may include anything from a specific age group/life stage to racial/cultural background, gender/sexual orientation, or marriage/partnership status. You can choose electives geared to your population of interest or learn about groups with which you are not familiar to increase your respect for diversity.

- **Do you plan to pursue a particular specialty?** You may want to work with specific issues or specialize in a particular technique, such as brief therapy, Gestalt or cognitive/behavioral. Electives can help you prepare for your special focus, and this additional training will increase your skills and credibility when you move out into the professional world.

Other Tracks of Study

Many schools offer other tracks of study for students who wish to become professional counselors in a certain field such as school counseling, substance abuse counseling, community counseling or marital and family therapy. These tracks will include classes focused on a specialized topic. Students simply follow the pre-defined track instead of choosing general elective courses.

PRACTICUM/INTERNSHIP

CACREP standards require students to complete a practicum and internship as a mandatory part of their degree program. These are both hands-on work experiences in which a student works without pay in exchange for on-the-job experience and supervision. The practicum and internship may be served in virtually any mental health service environment, but the job should reflect a student's professional interests and program of study.

Not only does this requirement prepare the student to enter the working world, but it also helps her to confirm that she's making the right career choice and choosing a comfortable area in which to focus. If she's still undecided, it will help her narrow her choices through direct experience.

The Practicum

The practicum in a CACREP-accredited program requires students to earn a minimum of 100 clock hours of experience over a 10-week school term. At least 40 of those hours must be spent providing direct services to clients. This allows students to develop and practice their theoretical counseling skills. They must also spend an average of one hour each week in supervision with a site supervisor, student supervisor, or faculty member. In addition, they must undergo an average of 90 minutes per week of group supervision with a faculty member or student supervisor.

The way in which the student carries out her counseling duties is continually evaluated throughout the course of the practicum. She gets feedback on her overall performance, including both strengths and weaknesses. She'll also get a formal evaluation at the end of the practicum period.

The Internship

Students in CACREP accredited programs must complete an internship in their area of study once they have successfully made it through their practicum. This runs for 600 hours and provides the student with work experience within her chosen counseling field. Of the total hours, at least 240 must be spent in providing direct services to clients, which can include both individual and group work. The student must also undergo an average of one hour per week of individual supervision and an average of 90 minutes per week of group supervision. In addition to working with clients, students learn about related tasks in the counseling field, such as using test and assessments, record keeping, and participating in staff meetings.

As in the practicum, the student's performance in their internship will be continually evaluated to determine what she's doing well and where she needs improvement. A formal evaluation is done at the end of the program.

Finding a Practicum/Internship Position

When you search for a position, you'll get a small taste of what it will be like to search for your permanent job. Even though you'll be volunteering your services, you'll still have to go through an interview process to be accepted for most practicums and internships. Some agencies, particularly those that are affiliated with the government, may also require you to undergo a background check.

Landing a practicum or internship position will be easier than landing a permanent job because it's a volunteer position. Still, while the odds are in your favor, there is no guarantee that you'll be accepted. Many job sites only accept a limited number of student workers each semester. Even though they're not paying a salary, they're committing to provide a certain level of supervision and the accompanying paperwork. They can't take on more volunteers than they can adequately supervise. Because of this possibility, you should be ready to apply to multiple sites.

To locate potential practicum or internship sites, talk to your instructors, the program director, or your university's career counselor. They often have lists of agencies that are actively seeking student interns.

Another good source of job leads is to contact local social service agencies and non-profit organizations. These sites often welcome student interns as a way to provide community services while functioning on a limited budget.

Before taking a practicum or internship position, make sure that a qualified supervisor will be available and that she is willing to meet with you in accordance with the CACREP requirements and provide the necessary evaluations.

Personal Insight

FROM THE AUTHOR: I served my practicum at a social service agency, and working with clients in the real world was a huge leap from studying theories and acting out role plays in a classroom. Along with my fellow students, I had watched videotaped sessions and practiced various techniques. It always felt unnatural, and I wondered if it would really work when I had a real person with a concrete issue sitting across from me and counting on me to help.

I remember practicing Rogerian techniques and active listening skills with classmates. It felt so awkward to try to find spots to interject neutral feedback like, "Yes, I see," or "Umm hmm," as the other person spoke. When I was doing the same thing with a real client, would he look at me as though I was crazy?

During my practicum, I nervously put my newly-minted skills to work. I was relieved and gratified when clients responded very well to my attentive listening. They seemed to relax and open up more. I tried other techniques and those seemed to work, too. I realized that I was seeing the melding of theory with hands-on application.

It's one thing to have a book or professor tell you, "Theory A works and this is why." It's quite another to see it happening when you're taking an active role with a real client. My practicum was the turning point that gave me confidence and showed me I could use all those years of schooling out in the professional world.

PSI-CHI MEMBERSHIP

Many colleges and universities have a chapter of Psi Chi, the National Honor Society in Psychology. Graduate students who wish to join must be enrolled in a psychology program and have an overall grade point average of at least 3.0 on a 4.0 scale. Psi Chi is also open to undergraduates who are at least a second-semester sophomore and are majoring or minoring in psychology or an equivalent topic. They must also meet the appropriate GPA requirements.

Psi Chi provides a support system and networking opportunities for students who share a common goal. It also gives research grants and various chapter and advisor awards. More information can be found on their website at www.psichi.org.

TRADITIONAL SCHOOLS VS. ONLINE PROGRAMS

Although the idea of college usually conjures up visions of a sprawling campus dotted with ivy-covered buildings, there many accredited counseling programs that can be completed online, with no need to ever set foot in a classroom. Some traditional colleges offer online classes as a complement to their "regular" programs, but a true online school grants degrees that are earned entirely on the internet.

Online degrees continue to gain acceptance among potential employers. In a 2008 survey by Vault.com, a media company focused on careers and human resources, 83 percent of hiring professionals said that online degrees had become more acceptable than they were just five years prior, and almost half had encountered job applications whose degrees were earned entirely online.

Accreditation of Online Schools

The same six bodies that accredit bricks-and-mortar schools will also give accreditation to online colleges and universities that meet their quality standards. You may find some online schools that say they are accredited by the Distance Education Training Council (DETC). The DETC is a legitimate organization with high standards, but its accreditation is not as universally accepted as that of the six regional agencies.

To ensure that your degree will meet licensure and employer standards, choose an online school with regional accreditation or check with your state's licensing board. If you're planning to take online classes from a DETC, accredited school and transfer them to a traditional college, make sure that they will be accepted if the online school doesn't also have regional accreditation.

To check any online school's accreditation status, visit the Council for Higher Education Accreditation's database at www.chea.org/search/default. asp. Even if a college claims to be accredited, it's always a good idea to verify this information at the source. While most online colleges are above-board, there are some unscrupulous "diploma mills" that try to lure students under false pretenses. These will be discussed in more depth later in this chapter.

Benefits and Drawbacks of Online Schools

Just like traditional colleges, online schools have their pros and cons. Always weigh these carefully when making a decision on where and how to earn your degree.

Online degrees continue to gain acceptance among potential employers.

Pros

- **Flexible Schedules.** Online schools typically allow students to complete work on their own schedule because there are no set hours. This makes them ideal for people who are working while attending school or adults who are juggling classes with family and job responsibilities.
- **Affordability.** Many online programs are less expensive than their traditional counterparts. Online schools have lower overhead and expenses, which they can pass along to their students. They also eliminate the expense of commuting or living on campus.
- **Self Pacing.** In an online class, students can work at their own pace as long as they keep up with the minimum requirements. If you are a fast learner, you can complete your work more quickly and earn your degree in an accelerated timeframe. You won't be held back as you would be in a traditional classroom, where everyone must follow the same schedule. On the flipside, if you're a slow, deliberate worker, you won't feel any pressure as long as you can complete your work by the deadline.
- **Zero Travel Time.** Because you will be taking your classes at home, you don't have travel to a campus, using up time and gasoline. You won't have to go through the hassle of finding a parking spot and hiking through the lot in the rain or snow. Just turn on your computer, sit down at the keyboard, and plunge into your schoolwork.
- **No Geographic Limitations.** If you live in a small town or isolated region, you won't have to drive a long distance or live on a campus in order to attend a quality school. As long as you have an internet connection, you'll have your choice of several accredited programs that are of the same caliber as comparable in-person schools.

Cons

- **Loss of Motivation.** If you're not disciplined, it's easy to fall behind in an online program because you don't have the commitment of a class that meets regularly and an instructor who can pressure you in-person if you don't turn in assignments. As you slip farther behind in your work, your motivation might evaporate. In the worst case, if you get too far behind, you might give up on your whole program.
- **Lack of Personal Attention.** In a traditional school, you can ask questions and speak to your instructor one-on-one during or after class or at regularly scheduled office hours. While online instructors make themselves available via email and phone, you won't have regularly scheduled interaction time and there may be a delay in their response.
- **Isolation:** If you're an extrovert who draws energy from having others around you and interacting with classmates, it may be draining to work

alone in front of your computer. Unlike a college campus, you won't have opportunities for social interaction, forming study groups, and listening to the questions and classrooms discussions initiated by other students. You may be able to interact online via forums and chat rooms, but it's not the same dynamic as talking face to face.

- ***Dependence on Computer/Internet.*** In order to complete your work, you'll need a computer and reliable internet connection. If your computer crashes and it takes a while to get a replacement or if you have problems with your internet service provider, you will fall behind in your schoolwork. You must be diligent in backing up your files so you don't lose that term paper in a computer crash before you turn it in.

DIPLOMA MILL WARNING

It looks too good to be true. You just received an email touting master's degrees that can be earned in as little as a week. For the low, low price of $149, you can get an M.A. in counseling psychology based on your "life experience." The school, State of Arizona University, claims to be fully accredited by the North Center Association. Your spidey sense is tingling, and it's right on the mark. This solicitation is full of red flags that mark it as the work of a diploma mill.

If you have an email account, you've probably received similar offers promising a degree with little or no work. They come from dubious institutions commonly known as "diploma mills" because they crank out credentials to anyone who will pay. Often there is no pretense of any actual schoolwork. Some do claim to require classes, but the duration is so brief and the work is so easy that anyone can pass. Most often, they simply claim to award you "life experience credit" and give you a degree on that basis. Your diploma arrives within weeks, or even days, as long as your payment has cleared.

Unfortunately, that degree was probably printed in someone's spare bedroom on their laser jet printer, and it's not even worth the toner they used to produce it. No state licensing agency will accept it to fulfill educational requirements, and it can't be transferred to any other school. There's no shortcut to a legitimate education, and you'll waste money and effort if you fall for pitches that claim to offer one.

Diploma Mill Tricks

Diploma mills use many tricks to appear legitimate. Let's use the example from the beginning of the chapter to expose some typical tactics.

- ***Deceptive Naming.*** Some diploma mills christen themselves with a name that is similar to a legitimate university. For example, they might dub themselves "North-Western" or "Notre Dane." In the earlier example, we have a school calling itself "State of Arizona University." That isn't much different than Arizona State University or University of Arizona, both of which are legitimate schools.

Double check the name and location of any online school you're considering. Be sure you're searching for information on the correct school, not some purposely misleading variation.

- **Worthless Accreditation.** Many degree mills claim to be accredited, but if you investigate the accreditation agency, you'll discover that it's not recognized by any other school or licensing board. Usually it's a creation of the school itself and exists only in the virtual world, although its name might be similar to that of a legitimate agency.

  In the example, the diploma mill claims to be accredited by the North Center Association. This name is similar enough to the North Central Association to trick potential students who are too dazzled by the offer to scrape below the surface.

  The diploma mill simply makes up the accreditation agency and throws together a website. The connection isn't disclosed, but the site often looks amazingly similar to that of the school itself. They might even be hosted by the same web company or registered to the same entity if you search for their domain registration information.

  Some diploma mills don't even go through the trouble of creating their own agency. They claim to be accredited by a legitimate, recognized organization, hoping that prospective students won't check. A search of the Council for Higher Education Accreditation database will quickly reveal the ruse.

- **An Extremely Low Flat Fee.** Real colleges charge their tuition based on credit hours, not a flat fee like the $149 quotes in the example email. A graduate degree costs thousands of dollars, even at a legitimate online university, and there's no way to avoid paying unless you get a scholarship or grant. If you buy a degree for a ridiculously low price, you'll find yourself living the cliché "you get what you pay for" when you try to use it with a state licensing board or potential employer.

- **Little or No Coursework Required.** The purpose of attending college is to gain the knowledge and experience required to work as a professional counselor. The coursework should be rigorous because you're learning new information. Diploma mills that claim to require classes often award a degree based on one or two papers that anyone could write. Obviously they're not concerned about preparing you for a career. They want you to "finish school" as quickly as possible so they can cash your check, send your degree, and move on to the next victim.

Some diploma mills don't even pretend to make you do any work. They award your degree based on "life experience," which always seems to qualify with no additional effort on your part other than sending a payment. An effortless degree is worthless for any professional use because you won't gain any of the necessary knowledge or skills.

How to Protect Yourself

If you follow a few simple guidelines, you'll protect yourself from diploma mills:

- Never respond to a college or diploma-related spam email or click through an online university ad that makes unrealistic promises
- *Disregard any school that claims to award degrees in an unrealistic timeframe
- Disregard any school that claims to award degrees based mostly or completely on life experience
- Disregard any school that offers a flat rate for their degree program, especially if the amount is unrealistically low

CHAPTER SUMMARY

- Professional counselors are required to earn a master's degree.
- High school students should prepare for college by taking psychology and other appropriate classes, participating in career day activities, earning high grades, seeking financial aid, and applying to appropriate schools.
- Many colleges have a formal evaluation process for homeschooled students.
- College students applying to graduate school should choose an accredited college and program.
- Graduate programs require core classes, electives, and completion of a practicum and internship.
- When considering an online degree program, prospective students should ensure that the school and its program are both accredited by a legitimate agency.
- Prospective students should avoid online diploma mills that sell worthless degrees for little money and no effort.

THE LICENSURE PROCESS

O nce you graduate with your master's degree, the next step on the road to becoming a professional counselor is to apply for your state license. This is not as simple as filling out a few forms, paying the required fee, and being handed a piece of official paper. Although the requirements vary from state to state, in addition to an appropriate degree they typically include some form of the following:

- Completion of a specified number of hours of post-master's supervised clinical experience which must be completed in a specified time period. For example, you might be required to earn 3000 hours of experience and to complete it within 24 months.
- Passage of either the National Counselor Examination (NCE) and/ or the National Clinical Mental Health Counselor Examination (NC-MHCE).

Once you have completed those requirements and received your counseling license, you will typically be required to:

- Adhere to professional standards of practice and a code of ethics as spelled out by your state's licensing board.
- Periodically complete continuing education classes. Your state board may dictate that these classes are to be on specific subjects or they may allow you to choose the topic.

Let's look at these requirements in a little more depth:

WORKING UNDER SUPERVISION

The first task you will face in the pursuit of your counseling license is to find a job where you can gain supervised experience. You'll have to complete the number of hours required by your state board, and your supervisor must verify this. At this point, you will most likely have initiated the licensing process and may have a designation such as registered intern or provisional counselor. The specific title will vary by state, but it means that you can legally provide counseling services as long as you're doing so under supervision. You will maintain this status until you complete all of your state's requirements to qualify for full licensure.

Nancy J. Razza, a licensed psychologist and supervisor in New Jersey, says there are two core goals of supervision: 1) Helping a graduate learn how to integrate academic understanding with the unique needs and presentation of the person sitting before them; and 2) Helping a graduate to become aware of, and examine, their own emotional reactions to their work with a given individual. Both of these goals are critical to preparing a new counselor for an independent practice.

Post-graduation supervision is somewhat different than what you receive in your school program. When you're going through your practicum in school, on-the-job supervision is typically supplemented by group discussions in the classroom. Although you will get one-on-one mentoring from your supervisor, you'll also have input from your instructors and fellow students. This additional feedback ends once you're done with school.

When you receive your degree and begin the process of obtaining a license to practice as a professional counselor, supervisions will take on a new level of importance. Most states require a new graduate to work under supervision for a specified number of hours before she is allowed to practice on her own. There will no longer be an instructor and fellow students to rely on. In the working world, your supervisor becomes your main support system, mentor, and quality control person.

What exactly does supervision entail? It might bring up visions of an employee/boss relationship, but in the context of counseling a supervisor is more of a mentor/guide/sounding board. She will share her professional experience and opinions with you and analyze your performance to help you treat your clients more effectively.

A good supervisor will aim to provide a safe, caring environment in which you can openly discuss your work and any concerns or problems you might be facing.

During your supervision sessions, you will discuss your approach in treating your current clients, including specifics of the sessions and any problems you might be encountering. Clients are notified before beginning treatment that you will be discussing them during supervision so they can either provide their informed consent or opt not to proceed. Most clients have no problem with supervision because it's a way of ensuring that they are receiving the best possible service.

Your supervisor will typically be an individual who has met educational and licensure requirements and practiced for a certain number of years. Some states require additional qualifications such as classes in supervision. When you are choosing a facility in which to do your practicum or complete your required hours of experience, be sure that you'll be working with a qualified supervisor who meets your school's or states requirements. You don't want to rack up dozens of work hours, only to discover that they don't count towards your license.

A good supervisor will aim to provide a safe, caring environment in which you can openly discuss your work and any concerns or problems you might be facing. You must trust your supervisor and feel comfortable with her in order to be able to share freely. When you're seeking a position and going through interviews, make sure that you and your potential supervisor "click." Although it's hard to tell in a brief meeting, go with your gut feeling.

Students and new counselors may be afraid to fully open up to their supervisor for fear of sounding "dumb" or being told that they're taking a totally wrong approach. Anxieties are common for anyone just starting out in the field. A supervisor isn't there to judge but rather to help her charges honestly evaluate their strengths and weaknesses. Then the strengths can be built on and the weaknesses can be replaced with a more effective approach.

Finding a Supervisor

When looking for your first job, make sure that you'll be working for someone who means your state's specific requirements to act as your supervisor. In many locations, not all licensed mental health professionals are automatically qualified to provide supervision. Each state's board will have its own requirements, which may include a certain amount of professional experience and additional training in effective supervisory techniques. If you're not sure about a potential supervisor's status, you should be able to verify that they're qualified through your state board, either online or via a phone call or letter.

If your immediate boss would not be a qualified supervisor, there may be someone else within the agency or organization who is willing and able to take on that role. Make sure that there is an agreement to provide you with supervision that falls within your state's guidelines before you accept any position.

A Supervisor's Role

A supervisor acts as a mentor, discussing your methods and approach with clients and how you might be able to improve them. Supervision gives you on-the-job training, but with a twist. Because counseling sessions are between you and your client, you'll be self-reporting and using your own notes during supervisory meetings.

Your supervisor will generally do the following:
- Listen to descriptions of your sessions and your questions and concerns
- Offer face-to-face guidance, feedback and mentoring
- Document your work hours
- Send appropriate paperwork to the licensing board

What to Expect From Your Supervisor

There are several things that a student or new counselor should expect from her supervisor. These include:
- An appropriate amount of time. At a minimum, the supervisor should be able to provide the number of hours required by the school program or the state licensing board. She should also be available if you need help at other times.
- Non-judgmental support. The student or new counselor should feel free to talk about virtually anything, including concerns and anxieties. While a good supervisor will make suggestions if she feels that changes are needed, she must do this a non-accusatory way. In a sense, she is modeling several of the traits of a healthy therapeutic relationship.
- Guidance. A supervisor is a mentor. Her role is to share her knowledge and experience with those who are new to the field, enabling them to benefit from that experience and to advance more quickly in their own professional growth. A good supervisor is willing to share what she knows and help her charges to adapt it into their own work, but she still allows them to maintain their own style.

 *Personal Insight*

Psychologist Nancy J. Razza feels that supervision is key to the growth and development of the professional. She says, "In supervision, the student has the opportunity to sit with an experienced professional and reflect on how what he or she has learned relates to a given case. She can consider different ways of understanding a particular personality or way of behaving, as well as sort through the risks and benefits of different strategies she might try.

"An old maxim in the field states that 'complex problems require complex solutions'; there is no cookbook response for any problem severe enough to get a person to go into counseling. The application of a body of clinical knowledge to the unique presentation of the individual sitting in front of the student is an art as much as a science. It may sound trite to say so, but it is an important truth."

She adds, "Inevitably, when we do counseling, our own feelings are triggered. We may feel annoyed by a client, or we may find ourselves wishing we could protect them. Perhaps we overextend ourselves for some clients, and put off calling others back. Our emotional reactions are important sources of information about ourselves and about our clients. But it typically takes the objectivity of a supervisor, and her extensive clinical expertise, to help a supervisee tease apart what part is his (and requires him to raise his own awareness), and what part is his client's."

EXAMS

Virtually every state requires applicants for a counseling license to pass a comprehensive examination. State boards typically use the NCE, the NCMHCE or both, and the National Board for Certified Counselors (NBCC) handles administration of these tests. For more information, including specific state requirements, test dates/locations and study guides, visit the NBCC website at http://sbv.nbcc.org/stateexamination.

The NCMHCE

The NCMHCE tests a counselor's ability to apply knowledge in real world clinical situations rather than simply regurgitating memorized facts in an objective format. It presents ten simulated cases that require the applicant to identify, analyze, diagnose and create a treatment plan. The cases are based on common clinical issues that a real client might present. Applicants must also demonstrate familiarity with the ethical and legal issues surrounding professional counseling.

The NCE

The NCE tests a counselor's objective knowledge in various areas related to professional counseling. It consists of 200 multiple choice questions in the areas of human growth and development; social and cultural foundations; helping relationships; working with groups; career and lifestyle development; appraisal; research and program evaluation; and professional orientation and ethics. This test is meant to be broad enough to measure the general knowledge that any counselors should possess, no matter what specialty she plans to enter.

Preparing for the Exams

Both the NCMHCE and the NCE test exam takers on knowledge that they should have acquired in college. The NCE tests the objective facts and theories that are typically covered in the classroom, while the NCHHCE tests the practical applications that should have been learned during the practicum. Because their licensure hinges on passing the appropriate exam, many applicants feel more comfortable brushing up on the related topics and skills before they sit for the test, even if they've been through a sound college program.

The NBCC, which administers the exams, maintains a web page listing preparatory courses and materials provided by third-party vendors. While the NBCC does not endorse specific vendors or guarantee the quality or accuracy of their preparatory material, this page is a handy resource for exam takers. It can be found at http://sbv.nbcc.org/study.

PROFESSIONAL TITLES

Once you qualify for and receive your license, you'll be allowed to practice as a professional counselor without any supervisory oversight. Some licensed counselors do continue to work with a supervisor for their own personal enrichment, but it's not required.

Your exact licensed title will vary depending on the state in which you're working. The most commonly used titles are:
- Licensed Professional Counselor (LPC)
- Licensed Professional Counselor - Mental Health (LPCMH)
- Licensed Mental Health Counselor (LMHC)
- Licensed Professional Clinical Counselor (LPCC)
- Licensed Independent Mental Health Practitioner (LIMHP)
- Licensed Professional Counselor/Mental Health Service Provider (LPC/MHSP).

As of this writing, 49 of the 50 United States and the District of Columbia require counselors to be licensed. A person who tries to practice and uses the word "counselor" or "therapist" in his title without having a license can be subject to sanctions.

As of 2009, California was the only state in the U.S. that did not require a counseling license, but efforts were underway to change that. Most likely California will institute licensing of mental health counselors by the state's Board of Behavioral Sciences, which already licenses educational psychologists, marriage and family therapists, and social workers. Updates can be found on the board's website at www.bbs.ca.gov.

STATE AGENCIES THAT LICENSE COUNSELORS

Each state that requires counselors to be licensed has a bureau or board to handle this process. Because contact names and addresses can change, it's best to visit the website of the appropriate state agency in order to find the most current information.

Here are the websites for each state, as well as the District of Columbia:

Alabama (LPC): Alabama Board of Examiners in Counseling, www. abec.alabama.gov

Alaska (LPC): Board of Professional Counselors Division of Corporations, Business and Professional Licensing, www.dced.state.ak.us/occ/ppco. htm

Arizona (LPC): Arizona Board of Behavioral Health Examiners, www. bbhe.state.az.us

Arkansas (LPC): Arkansas Board of Examiners in Counseling, www. state.ar.us/abec

California: Board of Behavioral Sciences, www.bbs.ca.gov (has no licensing requirement as of 2008 but efforts are underway to institute one)

Colorado (LPC): State Board of Licensed Professional Counselor Examiners, www.dora.state.co.us/registrations

Connecticut (LPC): State of Connecticut Dept of Public Health, www. ct-clic.com

Delaware (LPCMH): Board of Professional Counselors of Mental Health, http://dpr.delaware.gov/

Florida (LMHC): Board of Clinical Social Work, Marriage and Family Therapy, and Mental Health Counseling, www.doh.state.fl.us/mqa/491

Georgia (LPC): Professional Licensing Board Examination Development and Testing Unit, www.sos.state.ga.us/plb/counselors

Hawaii LMHC): Department of Commerce and Consumer Affairs, www.hawaii.gov/dcca/areas/pvl/programs/mental

Idaho (LCPC): State Counselor Licensing Board Bureau of Occupational Licenses, www.ibol.idaho.gov/cou.htm

Illinois (LCPC): Department of Financial & Professional Regulation Division of Professional Regulation, www.dpr.state.il.us

Indiana (LMHC): Indiana Social Worker, Marriage and Family Therapist, and Mental Health Counselor Board, Indiana Professional Licensing Agency, www.in.gov/pla/bandc/mhcb/licen_mhc.html

Iowa (LMHC): Bureau of Professional Licensure, Board of Behavioral Science, www.idph.state.ia.us/licensure/board_home.asp?board=be

Kansas (LCPC): Behavioral Sciences Regulatory Board, www.ksbsrb.org

Kentucky (LPCC): Kentucky Board of Licensed Professional Counselors, http://finance.ky.gov/ourcabinet/caboff/oas/op/procoun/

Louisiana (LPC): Licensed Professional Counselors Board of Examiners, www.lpcboard.org

Maine (LCPC): Maine Board of Counseling Professionals, www.state. me.us/pfr/olr/categories/cat13.htm

Maryland (LCPC): State of Maryland Dept. of Health and Mental Hygiene Board of Professional Counselors and Therapists, www.dhmh.state.md.us/bopc/

Massachusetts (LMHC): Board of Registration of Allied Mental Health and Human Services Professionals, www.mass.gov/reg/boards/mh

Michigan (LPC): Department of Community Health, www.michigan.gov/mdch

Minnesota (LPCC): Minnesota Board of Behavioral Health and Therapy, www.bbht.state.mn.us/

Mississippi (LPC): Mississippi State Board of Examiners for Licensed Professional Counselors, www.lpc.state.ms.us

Missouri (LPC): Division of Professional Registration Committee for Professional Counselors, www.pr.mo.gov

Montana (LCPC): Department of Labor and Industry Board of Social Work Examiners & Professional Counselors Dept. of Commerce Professional and Occupational Licensing Division, www.swpc.mt.gov

Nebraska (LIMHP): Nebraska Board of Mental Health Practice, www.hhs.state.ne.us/crl/mhcs/mental/mentalhealth.htm

Nevada (LCPC): Board of Examiners for Marriage and Family Therapists and Clinical Professional Counselors, http://marriage.state.nv.us/licensing.htm

New Hampshire LCMHC): New Hampshire Board of Mental Health Practice, www.state.nh.us/mhpb/

New Jersey (LPC): New Jersey Division of Consumer Affairs State Board of Marriage & Family Therapy Examiners, Professional Counselor Examiners Committee, www.state.nj.us/lps/ca/medical/familytherapy.htm

New Mexico (LPCC): New Mexico Therapy Practice Board Regulation and Licensing Dept., www.rld.state.nm.us/b&c/counseling/index.htm

New York (LMHC): State Board for Mental Health Practitioners State Education Department Office of the Professions, www.op.nysed.gov/mhp.htm

North Carolina (LPC): North Carolina Board of Licensed Professional Counselors, www.ncblpc.org

North Dakota (LPCC): North Dakota Board of Counselor Examiners, www.ndbce.org

Ohio (LPCC): Ohio Counselor Social Worker, Marriage & Family Therapist Board, http://cswmft.ohio.gov/

Oklahoma (LPC): Licensed Professional Counselors Advisory Board

Oklahoma State Department of Health, www.health.ok.gov/program/lpc

Oregon (LPC): Oregon Board of Licensed Professional Counselors and Therapists, www.oblpct.state.or.us

Pennsylvania (LPC): State Board of Social Workers, Marriage and Family Therapists and Professional Counselors, www.dos.state.pa.us/bpoa/cwp/view.asp?a=1104&q=433177

Rhode Island (LCMHC): Board of Mental Health Counselors and Marriage & Family Therapists, Rhode Island Department of Health Professions Regulation, www.healthri.org/hsr/professions/mf_counsel.php

South Carolina (LPC): South Carolina Department of Labor Licensing Regulations, Division of Professional and Occupational Licensing, www.llr.state.sc.us/pol/counselors

South Dakota (LPCMH): South Dakota Board of Counselor Examiners, www.dhs.sd.gov/brd/counselor

Tennessee (LPC): Tennessee State Board of Licensed Professional Counselors, Marital and Family Therapists and Licensed Pastoral Therapists, http://health.state.tn.us/Boards/PC_MFT&CPT/

Texas (LPC): Texas State Board of Examiners of Professional Counselors, www.dshs.state.tx.us/counselor

Utah (LPC): Department of Occupational Professional Licensing, www.dopl.utah.gov/licensing/professional_counselor.html

Vermont (LCMHC): Secretary of State's Office Board of Allied Mental Health Practitioners, http://vtprofessionals.org/opr1/allied/

Virginia (LPC): Virginia Board of Professional Counselors Dept of Health Professionals, www.dhp.virginia.gov

Washington State (LMHC): Health Professions Quality Assurance, Washington State Department of Health, www.doh.wa.gov

Washington D.C. (LPC): Department of Health, Health Regulation and Licensing Administration (HRLA), www.doh.dc.gov

West Virginia (LPC): West Virginia Board of Examiners in Counseling, www.wvbec.org

Wisconsin (LPC): Wisconsin Department of Regulation Licensing, http://drl.wi.gov/prof/coun/def.htm

Wyoming (LPC): Mental Health Professions Licensing Board, http://plboards.state.wy.us/mentalhealth/index.asp

WHERE DO YOU PLAN TO PRACTICE?

If you already know the state in which you plan to practice counseling, or if you've narrowed down your choices to two or three states, use the websites provided in this section to do a little research. Knowing the requirements ahead of time can save you frustration and delays in the licensure process later.

For each state you're considering, make a page with the following headings: Responsible Agency, Educational Requirements, Experience Requirements, Examination, Additional Requirements, Provisional Licensing, Supervision, and Continuing Education Requirements. This will be your worksheet.

Next, visit the state's website and download an application for licensure and any other information that might be provided. Use this to find the specific requirements for each of the categories and fill in your sheet with as much detail as possible. This will give you a handy comparison tool, and if you've already settled on your practice location it will give you a checklist as you work your way through the process.

PORTABILITY OF COUNSELING CREDENTIALS

At present there is no accepted standard for portability of counseling credentials from state to state. Because of this, you will need to apply for a new license if you move your practice from one state to another or if you live near a border and wish to practice in two different states.

The American Association of State Counseling Boards (AASCB) is working to develop common standards that will allow for nationwide portability of professional counseling licenses. While this is still a work in progress, you can find the latest information on their website at www.aascb.org.

 *Personal Insight*

FROM THE AUTHOR: I didn't apply for my license immediately after earning my master's degree. I continued to work under supervision at the social service agency where I'd done my internship. Then we moved to another state and I was finally ready to apply for my license.

My master's program wasn't CACREP accredited, and I'd taken the industrial psychology track in order to qualify for my employer's tuition reimbursement program. This meant that I was missing several classes required by the state licensing board. Fortunately I met enough of the educational requirements to get my provisional license. This allowed me to practice under supervision while taking the missing classes and preparing for the NCMHCE.

During the application process, I learned one very important thing: keep copies of everything you send to the state board and every piece of correspondence. I had to order copies of my college transcripts, and because I'd done my practicum and earned some experience out of state I had to get my old employer to fill out a variety of forms. My former supervisor had left the social service agency, so I had to find someone to verify my hours in his stead.

All of this documentation arrived in trickles, and I dutifully forwarded it on to the state board. Periodically I would call or email to check on the status of my application and they'd say that some particular piece of documentation was missing. I'd check my files and see that I'd already sent it, but it was often easier to just send out another copy.

The provisional license was a Godsend because it allowed me to work as a counselor, as long as I did so under a supervisor, while taking the remaining classes at my leisure instead of being rushed to complete them. It also removed the pressure of having a looming deadline for the NCMHCE. I could finish my classes first, and then turn my full attention to preparing for the exam.

EXAMPLE: THE STATE OF FLORIDA

Even though states differ in their licensure requirements, there are some trends and similarities shared by most. Let's take a detailed look at the requirements laid out by the state of Florida for mental health counselors, since the Sunshine State is a fairly typical example. If you're planning to practice in a different state, you'll need to research its specific requirements. This example is meant as a generic to give you a general idea of what to expect.

Responsible Agency

The Florida Department of Public Health is the agency responsible for licensing counselors, as well as for handling licensure of similar professions. In Florida, this includes psychologists, marriage and family therapists, and clinical social workers. Other states typically handle licensing through their own public health departments or counseling-related boards or committees. However, some handle this process through their business, occupational, or professional licensing departments or boards. The list of websites given earlier in this chapter will guide you to the right entity for your own state.

Educational Requirements

The state of Florida requires all candidates for mental health counseling licensure to have earned a master's degree at an accredited school. Candidates must have majored in mental health counseling or an area closely related to the field. Ideally, the degree should have been earned in a CACREP-accredited mental health counseling program.

Applicants may obtain a mental health counseling license in Florida even if they went through a non-CACREP program. However, their program must meet the same requirements for semester or quarter hours as an accredited program. It must also include courses in eleven specific content areas: counseling theories and practice; human growth and development; diagnosis and treatment of psychopathology; human sexuality; group theories and practice; individual evaluation and assessment; career and lifestyle assessment; research and program evaluation; social and cultural foundations; counseling in community settings; and substance abuse. Coursework in legal, ethical and professional standards is also required.

The degree program, whether CACREP accredited or not, must include at least 1,000 hours of university-sponsored supervised clinical practicum, internship, or field experience as required in CACREP standards.

Experience Requirements

In addition to an appropriate degree, Florida requires candidates to earn two years of post-master's supervised experience in the mental health counseling field. This must take place under the direction of a qualified supervisor as spelled out in the Department of Public Health's requirements. During this process, the candidate should be registered as a mental health counseling intern as spelled out later in this chapter.

Supervision

In Florida, applicants must earn their post-graduate experience under a qualified supervisor as recognized by the state board. This must be done face-to-face, with both the supervisor and the intern being physically together in the same room. Sessions cannot be conducted over the telephone, online, or through any method other than an in-person meeting. Otherwise, they won't meet state requirements or count towards the required hours.

Provisional Licensing

If an applicant in Florida meets the educational and practicum/internship requirements, she can apply to become a Registered Mental Health Counseling Intern (RMHCI). This allows her to practice as a counselor while she completes the requirements for supervised experience and prepares to take the NCMHCE exam. She is required to work under a qualified supervisor during this period.

Most other states have their own form of provisional licensure or registration. The exact title varies, but it may refer to the applicant as an intern, a registered counselor, or the holder of a provisional or limited license. Registering as a mental health counseling intern required a fee of $150 in Florida as of 2009. Other states impose similar fees.

Examination

Applicants for a mental health counseling license in Florida must also pass the National Clinical Mental Health Counseling Examination (NCMHCE). Out of the two NBCC tests typically used by states to fulfill their licensure requirements, this one focuses on applied knowledge rather than memorization of objective facts. If you do not pass on your first try, the Florida licensing board allows you to take it again after a waiting period of 90 days. Most states have similar allowances for those who don't initially earn a passing score.

Additional Requirements

Applicants must also complete an eight-hour laws and rules course and a two-hour prevention of medical errors course. This requirement is specific to Florida, and these are not college courses. They must be taken from independent providers who have been approved by the licensing board. Other states may have their own unique requirements in a similar vein.

Application/Licensing Fee

The state of Florida requires applicants to pay an application fee and an initial licensure fee. As of 2009 these were $100 and $105 respectively, which is in line with the amounts typically charged by other states. You will need to apply for a renewal and pay this fee each year in order to keep your license current.

Continuing Education Requirements

The state of Florida requires mental health counselors to earn continuing education credits on an on-going basis. The exact requirements depend on the license renewal date, but they generally include courses in specific areas such as preventing medical errors, ethics and boundary issues, and domestic violence. Counselors must choose a state-approved provider from which to take these courses in order to make sure that their content fulfills the requirement.

CHAPTER SUMMARY

- The first step after graduation is to apply for a state license to practice counseling.
- Prospective counselors are typically required to gain supervised experience before they can be fully licensed.
- Most states require applicants for a counseling license to pass an exam, such as the NCE or the NCMHCE.
- Some states require additional training beyond the college degree.
- Applicants typically must pay an application and/or licensing fee and

renew their license regularly.
• Continuing education classes may be required as a condition of renewal.

YOUR JOB SEARCH

Once you are a licensed mental health counselor, you can begin your job search to find the position that is right for you. Your degree program, practicum, internship and supervised experience will have given you a good idea of the type of work you'd like to do as your long-term career. Now you must find opportunities that align with your preferences and focus on getting a well-matched job.

FINDING OPPORTUNITIES

There are many sources for mental health counseling positions. The most common places to find prospective employment include:

- Newspaper ads. Many mental health facilities and other organizations that hire counselors advertise in the classified section of their local newspaper. The Sunday edition typically contains a special ad section. Buy it and scan the relevant categories, making a note of any promising ads. Some will list the employer, while others may be "blind ads" that ask for a response to an anonymous post office box. If a blind ad looks attractive, don't be afraid to send your resume. If the employer turns out to be undesirable, you can simply withdraw yourself from consideration.
- Online ads. There are many dedicated job search websites such as Careerbuilder.com, Monster.com, Jobs.com and Indeed.com. Some general classified ad sites like Craigslist also include employment opportunities. All of these sites let you narrow your search to your local area and the surrounding vicinity and to specific topics and types of positions.

Many job sites also allow you to post your resume and advertise your availability to prospective employers. Unfortunately, this makes your personal information available to anyone who signs up for an account. Unscrupulous individuals and scammers may pose as prospective employers and gain access to your resume, then barrage you with worthless pitches.

They may contact you with phony job offers and tell you that you need to pay a fee in order to get complete information, or they may offer to sell you a list of "hot" opportunities. Some will offer jobs that are totally unrelated to the mental health field. Some harvest valid phone numbers from job sites, so you may find yourself receiving a flurry of telemarketing calls, while others gather email addresses for spam lists or to target for various scams.

While posting your resume may have some value, you must weigh the risks against the benefits. Many employers are too busy to sift through the thousands of resumes on job sites. They would rather place an ad and have prospective applicants respond to it because that's more efficient and convenient. You might miss some opportunities, but overall it shouldn't impact your job search too severely.

If you do decide to post your resume, there are two simple things you can do to protect yourself:

- Open an email account just for your job search. Use a free provider such as Gmail or Yahoo and choose a professional-sounding name. Email addresses like sexyylippz@yahoo.com don't tend to make a good first impression on prospective employers. Once you've gotten a job, close the account and you won't have to deal with the flood of spam.
- Get a disposable phone number just for your job search. Buy a cheap pay-as-you-go cell phone to field calls from prospective employers. When you get your new job, you can simply stop using the phone and you won't have to deal with any annoying telemarketers who pulled the number from your resume.

Government Jobs

If you're interested in a job with the federal government, visit their official website at www.usajobs.gov. Most states also have official websites detailing their employment opportunities and how to apply. A list of official state websites, which usually include links to official job information, can be found at www.usa.gov/Agencies/State_and_Territories.shtml. Never do business with anyone who claims that you must pay for government job listings or any other type of employment opportunities.

- **Networking.** During your schooling and practicum/internship, you've no doubt made some valuable connections. Potentially useful contacts include instructors, department heads, academic counselors, and other personnel at your college; fellow students in your counseling program; and co-workers and supervisors at your practicum/internship sites. If you have attended conferences and presentations, you may have made valuable contacts there, too. Use these connections to help you find job leads once you have achieved licensure. Besides pointing you towards potential employment, people in your network may be willing to give you a personal recommendation or reference.

- *Professional organizations.* Many professional organizations for counselors allow you to join at a discounted rate while you are a student. Depending on the organization, your membership may give you access to job listings and other employment-related resources. For example, the American Counseling Association (ACA) has a dedicated "Career Center" on its website which includes articles, a question and answer section, and job listings. If you don't already belong to organizations that offer these services, consider joining at least one when you're ready to start your job search.

- *College job placement office.* Your college may have a job placement office that posts updated employment opportunities and provides career counselors to assist graduates and alumni in their search. These services are usually provided at no cost, so make use of this resource if it is available.

- *Leg work.* Sometimes the best way to identify prospective employers is simply to do some legwork. Find as many potential job sites as you can through any means possible. This might include the phone book, online phone directories, service provider directories, or passing by a likely office or facility in your neighborhood. Even if those prospects aren't advertising any available jobs, you can still send them a resume. Many offices and agencies will keep resumes on file for a specified length of time, even if they're not hiring. When a position opens, they will scan the resumes they've collected to see if there are any promising candidates before they turn to advertising. This can give you an inside track if you have the right qualifications.

- *Professional Recruiters.* If your own job search is coming up dry, you may wish to turn to a professional recruiter. Never link up with a recruitment firm that asks you for a payment. Legitimate firms make their money from employers and get their payment once a candidate is successfully placed. If an individual or company claims to be a recruiter and solicits money from you, refuse to deal with them because they are most likely pulling a scam. Once they've pocketed your fee, they will have no incentive to find you a job and will most likely drop out of sight.

WHAT YOU WILL NEED

You'll need several important tools before you can embark on your job search:

- *A resume.* At a minimum, this document contains your personal information (name, address, phone number, and email address), career goal, professional experience, and educational background. It may also list special qualifications, honors/awards, and personal and/or professional references.

The purpose of a resume is to catch the eye of prospective employers and pique their interest. It's a quick summary that helps human resource professionals determine whether you're qualified enough to make it to the next step in the hiring process. It must be concise, yet offer enough detail to show them that you're worth a closer look.

When you're entering the field for the first time, you might be afraid that you don't have enough on-the-job experience to be taken seriously. Fortunately, your practicum, internship and supervised work experience during the licensure process will give you a solid work history. If you have supervisors or co-workers who are willing to provide references or letters of recommendation, this lends even more strength to your experience. Prospective employers look at quantity of prior work, but proven quality is just as important.

If you're not comfortable writing your resume, consult one of the many books and websites that offer guidance. Your college's placement office may offer free assistance, and you can also hire a professional. If you pay someone to assist, ask for samples of his work and references to check him out before you hire him.

You should be able to use one version of your resume for all prospective employers unless you are considering two or more specialized areas. For example, you might be looking for a job as a general mental health counselor, but you'll also consider positions that focus on substance abuse treatment. For the first option, you'd want a resume that stresses your general experience, showing that you've dealt with a wide range of clients and issues. For the second, you'd want to prepare another version that focuses on relevant experience with substance abusers, such as taking related electives or facilitating groups for alcoholics during your practicum. Each of those resumes would also feature a different version of your long-term goal.

- A cover letter that you can customize to send with resumes. This is simply a quick introduction that personalizes the contact and shows that you've done your homework. It should be addressed to a specific agency or organization and include the name of the appropriate hiring professional. It can be sent along with your resume via postal mail, email, or hand delivered.

  Never send out generic cover letters because this can indicate laziness on your part. If you're truly interested in a specific position, you should be willing to do enough research to find out the correct contact person. If you can find out some specific information about the office or agency, refer to that in the letter. For example, you might say, "I know that the Marlow Agency has been around for two decades and that you've recently expanded into the treatment of eating disorders. I have experience in that area, as you will see in my resume, so I believe I would be a good fit for your agency."

- A list of references. Although some job seekers include this on their resume, many others say, "Available upon request." If you don't include it, you should always have it on hand so you can provide it immediately when a prospective employer asks for it.

- Your references should include professionals who are familiar with your work performance, such as supervisors or co-workers, and instructors who can vouch for your college experience. Some employers will also want personal references. Pick people who have known you for a long time and are willing to give honest, detailed responses. You want them to give overall positive reviews, but not to the point of being unrealistic. When someone gives such a glowing review that it sounds too good to be true, it can raise red flags for the prospective employer.

MANAGING YOUR SEARCH

Your years of college and work experience will most likely have forced you to hone your time management and organizational skills. You can use these same skills to manage your job search effectively. An effective plan should include the following steps:

- ***Dedicate a certain amount of time each day to your job search.*** Until you are employed, your job search is basically your work. Give it the same time, attention and effort that you would devote to any other job. The more seriously you approach your search, the more successful you're likely to be.

- ***Have a specific search plan.*** This should include the amount of time you're going to spend on your search each day and the specific ways in which you will generate leads. You should also spell out a plan for following up on them promptly. This might include calling for more information, sending out a resume and cover letter, or visiting the job site to fill out an application.

- **Follow up immediately.** Whenever you get a nibble on a resume or expression of interest from a prospective employer, follow up as quickly as possible. This confirms your interest and enthusiasm, and it also prevents someone else from swooping in and grabbing the opportunity because you were too slow.

- **Don't get discouraged.** Many factors can cause you to have difficulty finding a job, and most don't have anything to do with you personally. Things like your local job market and the general economic climate all play in, and there is nothing you can do to control those influences. Don't waste time and energy worrying about rejections. Focus on the things you can control and channel your efforts into positive actions that support your job search.

- **Be flexible.** While it would be nice for your dream job to materialize immediately, that's probably not going to happen. Instead, you might have to take an interim position to earn more experience and pay the bills. Don't let this discourage you. View it as a stepping stone on the road to achieving your ultimate goal. Once you have a job that relieves financial stress, you can take your time as you search for a more ideal position.

In a way, your job search is like a class in school. Finding opportunities is like completing assignments. In a class you have to do a lot of assignments before you get to the final exam. In your quest for employment, you may have to work your way through many prospective jobs before you get called in for an interview. The interview is like that final exam. You may ace it the first time and get a "passing grade" in the form of a job offer. There's also a possibility that you'll "flunk," but once you complete some more assignments you'll get another chance.

PREPARING FOR AN INTERVIEW

Once you've piqued the interest of a prospective employer, the next step will most likely be to set up an in-person interview. Although there are general guidelines that apply to any type of employment interview, mental health-related positions have a few unique aspects. Being aware of these will help you prepare yourself in the best manner possible. They usually fall in the following areas:

- **Long-Term Goals:** When you are a licensed counseling professional, your goals should include the continuing education necessary to maintain your licensure. They might also include additional certifications in a specialized area such as an art-based therapy or group work. Be prepared to discuss these goals with the interviewer and to share concrete steps that you plan to take to achieve them.

- *Employer Culture:* Counseling positions can be found in a wide variety of environments. Depending on your focus, you'll be applying for a position in a group practice, social service agency, government office, in-patient or out-patient treatment facility, or school. Each of these employers has its own culture and environment. Becoming as familiar with these things as possible, and giving responses in the interview to show you understand them and would be a good fit, can boost your chances of getting the job.

- *Big Picture View:* Counseling is a job with far-reaching consequences. You're not just producing a product or providing a simple service like dry cleaning or pet grooming. You're working with people in a way that can have a deep impact on their lives. In your interview, you should show that you understand this big-picture view and that you know how your work fits into a greater whole. For example, if you're applying at a social service agency, be prepared to discuss how your work can potentially impact the surrounding community. If you're applying for a vocational counseling position, discuss how overall factors such as the job market and economy can affect your clients and how you plan to keep abreast of this information.

In addition to these special considerations, you should be prepared to demonstrate your work-specific knowledge. For example, an interviewer might ask the following types of questions:

- What specialized classes did you take in college?
- What was your favorite part of your previous counseling work, and why?
- What part did you dislike the most, and why?
- What is the biggest challenge you've faced in your work so far, and how did you handle it?
- How do you handle work-related stress?
- What is your biggest strength as a counselor, and how does it benefit you in your work?
- What is your biggest weakness as a counselor, and how to you offset it?

You may also be presented with a case and asked to discuss the type of treatment plan you would create and how you would work on it with the client. Some interviewers will present hypothetical examples of potentially challenging situations or ethical dilemmas and ask how you would handle them.

You'll never be able to prepare yourself for every possibility. Do the best you can, and if you're hit with a question that catches you by surprise, ask for a minute or two to formulate your answer. Most interviewers will respect the fact that it takes some time to consider difficult questions. Answer honestly and sincerely. If you're not sure about something, it's often best to go with your first thought or your gut feeling. If you get the job, fine. If you don't, it's a learning experience that will leave you better prepared to deal with the next interview.

OTHER REQUIREMENTS

If a potential employer likes you well enough to seriously consider hiring you, they may require any or all of the following:

- Additional Interviews. These may be with other professionals at the workplace who you haven't met before, or you might have a more focused an in-depth interview with someone who met with you previously.
- Background Checks. For many employers, a criminal record check is a standard part of their hiring procedure. This is especially true in jobs like counseling were employees provide hands-on services to clients. Many will also do a drug screening, and some will request a credit check. If you will be driving company vehicles or transporting clients, your driving record will be checked too. You will have to give your consent for these checks, but if you refuse it will most likely cost you the job offer.
- An Internet Search. More and more employers are plugging the names of prospective employees into an internet search engine. The candid information that pops up can be much more telling than any interview. Candidates are on their best behavior in an interview, but when they're posting to a blog or social network they tend to let out their true personality.

Be careful what you post on the internet. You may think those photos of you at the toga party look great on your MySpace or Facebook page, but will a hiring professional see them in the same humorous light? Even if you delete them, they can live on forever in archives or on other pages that are out of your control.

HANDLING JOB OFFERS

If your interview goes well and you pass all the other screenings required by a prospective employer, they will hopefully decide to extend a job offer. When this happens, you will probably feel elated because it means that all your hard work has finally paid off. All the years of schooling, the long hours of interning, and the voluminous licensure process have finally borne fruit.

Don't let your excitement cloud your logic. Just because you've gotten a job offer doesn't mean that you should automatically accept it. Look at it very closely, considering exactly what is being offered. Some common points include:

- What salary are you being offered, and is it within a fair range for the type of work, employer and location?
- Will you be paid hourly or receive a fixed salary?
- What are the hours you would have to work, and are they at all flexible? If it's a salaried position and you work extra hours, will you receive make-up time?
- What benefits will you receive, and how soon will they start? For example, if you're getting medical insurance and vacation time, is there a waiting period before you are eligible?
- Is there a clearly defined promotion path to give you the chance for advancement?
- Does the employer offer compensation for tuition for additional classes or seminars?
- Will the employer pay for your professional liability insurance? Do they contribute to professional memberships and foot the bill for conference attendance?
- Are the terms of the offer spelled out clearly in writing, and have they been confirmed by those with proper authority?

Usually there is room for negotiation within an employment offer. If most of the terms look good but there are one or two points of contention, make a counter offer. For example, if a prospective employer is only offering one week of vacation in the first year, you can ask if they will change it to two. If the pay rate is below the local standard, you can request a higher starting salary. If the employer insists on sticking to the initial offer, it's up to you to decide whether you can accept the terms or whether you'd rather look for a job with more compatible terms.

Personal Insight

Renee Murphy Hughes, LPC, a licensed mental health counselor practicing in North Carolina, says that she relied on word of mouth referrals, newspapers, and internet searches in order to find a job. However, a prime opportunity came as the result of professional connections. She explains, "The biggest job transformation for me in my career was really launched by a supervisor of mine that I was very close to and who took a special interest in me. At the time I was living in a rural part of North Carolina, and she saw a lot of potential in me and knew that if I was going to advance my career it was necessary that I move to a larger city with more job opportunities.

"During a state conference she attended, she met a couple of people who had secured a state grant for a family preservation project, and she put my name in for the position to head that project. She then came to me and told me about it even though it would require a move almost halfway across the state. I was very reluctant, with two children and a fiancé, but she really strongly encouraged me for the career advancement. My family and fiancé supported the move and I took it. I got the position and remained there for a long time."

CHAPTER SUMMARY

- Once you have received your license, the next step is your job search.
- You can find potential job opportunities through newspaper and online ads, networking, professional organizations, your college's placement department, and legwork.
- Beware of posting your resume online because your personal information may be harvested and used for other purposes.
- If you decide to use a professional recruiter to help you find a job, never pay an up-front fee. The employer should be the one to pay.
- Never pay money to obtain listings for government jobs or any other type of position.
- For your job search, you will need a resume, cover letter, and list of professional, educational and personal references.
- Your job search should be managed with the same care and dedication that you'd devote to your employment.
- When interviewing for a position in the mental health field, be prepared to discuss your long-term goals as related to job-specific development, how you would fit into a particular employer's culture, and how your work would fit into the big picture.
- Many employers will conduct background checks. These may include your criminal record, credit history, driving record, and a drug test. Some will also search your name on the internet for any potentially embarrassing references and links.
- Most job offers are negotiable, so ask for what you think is fair if you get an offer and it's lacking in some areas.
- If a prospective employer won't negotiate, your best bet might be to turn down the offer and concentrate your efforts on finding a more compatible position.

WORKING AS A MENTAL HEALTH COUNSELOR

As a professional mental health counselor, you won't be tossed in alone to sink or swim once you get your license and accept your permanent job. If you're working in a group practice or are employed by an office or agency, you'll have a supervisor and peer support. Even if you're working in private practice, you'll have tools you can use to assess clients and plan therapy sessions. You can also join professional organizations and take advantage of the networking opportunities and conferences sponsored by these groups.

PEER SUPPORT

Most counselors don't have to bear the burdens of their work alone. Unless you are in private practice, you'll have colleagues to whom you can turn for support and guidance. Peer support is somewhat different than "supervision." A supervisor typically evaluates performance as well as giving advice, while peer support is more of a consultation opportunity. Your peers offer their opinions objectively, without judgment, and you're free to use the information, ignore it, or choose some parts and disregard the rest.

Peer support has proven to be very effective for providing encouragement and helping counselors improve their techniques (Benshoff, 1992). In Bershoff's study, 86 percent of the participants rated consulting with their peers as being helpful. They acknowledged that it assists them in developing their counseling skills and increasing their understanding of professional concepts.

Even if you're working in your own office, you can find peers through professional groups like the American Counseling Association (ACA).

While the ACA is national in scope, it has many local divisions. Counselors in private practice can link up with others in their immediate area through these offshoots. They can also network at conferences and maintain a link with their new contacts once they have returned home.

If you don't have a formal supervisor because you have your own practice, you can retain someone to act in this role. Many state-qualified supervisors will provide supervision services to other professionals in addition to seeing clients their regular practice. Make sure that the person you choose has the proper experience and credentials and that their style is compatible with yours.

TOOLS OF THE TRADE

As a counselor, you won't have to come up with your treatment plans and strategies on the fly. Even though you have a master's degree, it's virtually impossible to remember everything that you were bombarded with in school and every bit of your practicum and internship. You may have had thorough training, but you'll still encounter unique cases and situations that will force you to draw upon other resources.

Professional counselors use a wide variety of tools to help them plan a client's treatment and assess his progress through the therapeutic process. There are many treatment planner books that contain suggested goals, steps and assignments for a variety of common emotional disorders and issues. Rather than having to create a document from scratch, you can use these books as a resource. Of course their generalized material must be customized for each client, but they give the therapist a solid framework on which to build a targeted plan.

Counselors also use a variety of assessment instruments to determine a client's current state of mind and whether there has been any progress or deterioration between sessions. There are a variety of scales to measure mental states such as depression, anxiety, and overall level of functioning. By having a client complete an assessment at the beginning of each session, the counselor has more information on his state of mind and can slant the session accordingly. When scores are compared with previous sessions, it also tells both client and counselor whether any progress is being made.

Peer support
has proven to be very effective
for providing
encouragement and helping counselors
improve their techniques

PROFESSIONAL ORGANIZATIONS

Because of the popularity of the counseling profession and its various specialties, there are a wide range of professional organizations that you can turn to for information and support. They typically provide networking opportunities, ethical guidelines, conferences, continuing education seminars, publications and other benefits.

One example is the American Counseling Association (ACA), a nonprofit organization for counselors, students, and anyone else who has an interest in the field. It offers membership tiers for qualified professionals, students, retirees, and others who might wish to join.

The ACA offers benefits typical of larger professional organizations. These include informational resources; state groups for licensed counselors; career assistance; a monthly magazine, an annual conference; a directory of member counselors; and affordable professional liability insurance.

Other professional associations focus on a specific job classification within the counseling field, a specific focus in treatment, or service of a particular group. For example, the Association for Behavioral and Cognitive Therapies (ABCT) provides information and networking opportunities for counselors who primarily use cognitive/behavioral techniques. The National Association of Adoption Counselors (NAAC) serves professionals who work with adoptive families, birth mothers and others involved in the adoption process. The Association for Death Education and Counseling (ADEC) supports counselors and other professionals who deal with death and bereavement. This is just a small sampling of the targeted organizations.

An association may also be specific to the counselor's own ethnicity or cultural background. For example, the Asian-American Psychological Association (AAPA) is aimed specifically at Asian- American mental health professionals. African-American counselors who offer Christian-based services can join the Black African-American Christian Counselors (BAACC).

The American Counseling Association itself offers many specialized divisions, such as the Association for Lesbian, Gay, Bisexual and Transgender Issues in Counseling (ALGBTIC) and the Association for Specialists in Group Work (ASGW).

A comprehensive list of professional organizations, including their web addresses, is included in the Resources section at the end of this book. You can also find associations tied to your areas of interest by running an internet search or asking colleagues. A list of American Counseling Association divisions can be found at www.counseling.org/AboutUs/DivisionsBranchesAndRegions/TP/Divisions/CT2.aspx.

Personal Insight

Nancy Williams, LPC, a licensed professional counselor practicing in Texas, finds great value in belonging to professional organizations. She says they offer two major benefits for her: "Some offer professional training to further my educational development and growth as a clinician. Many offer networking support, providing insight into how others are developing their businesses, marketing opportunities for my practice, and peer support through the development of relationships."

She also sees organizations as a way to give something back. She explains, "I've had the opportunity to give back to the community through organization-sponsored activities, fostering personal fulfillment and establishing a presence in the community."

It can be a challenge to choose the right association to join. Nancy says, "There are many professional organizations vying for attention. I look for a combination that together will offer a balance for me both personally and professionally. For example, my membership in the American Association of Christian Counselors provides professional continuing education. As a member of both the American Business Women's Association and Federation of Houston Professional Women, I can network with other professional women to enhance my business skills, market my practice, and foster personal relationships.

"My involvement as a professional representative in area organizations such as our school district's Educational Foundation and the Humble Area Assistance Ministries offers opportunities for me to volunteer in activities that create a visible presence and support in our community and also foster personal fulfillment for me.

"The field of counseling is both rewarding and challenging. In order to do what I do day after day, year after year, I must take care of my business and myself both personally and professionally. The organizations to which I belong play a major role in that focus."

ON THE JOB AS A COUNSELOR

A counselor's typical day can vary widely, depending on her workplace and specialization. For example, a school counselor will spend her day working with youngsters, while a rehabilitation counselor will be supporting disabled clients and a substance abuse counselor will be focused on helping addicts maintain their abstinence and sobriety. Even though each of these professionals is technically a counselor, they work with very different populations and focus on a wide variety of issues.

The pace of the day can vary too. Counselors in a private office or facility might have a more leisurely schedule than those who are working at a social service agency or government office where there is a major demand for service. Some workplaces, particularly those with lower pay scales, are chronically understaffed which can also contribute to a hectic workday.

A Typical First Appointment

One situation that is common to virtually any type of counseling is the initial appointment. Unless you're in a field where clients are typically screened and assessed by others, you'll do the initial screening yourself to determine what a person needs and if you can provide appropriate service. Even when you're dealing with pre-screened individuals, the initial appointment is a time to see if you and the client "click" and if he is comfortable with your approach.

Here is how a typical first appointment might go for a mental health counselor who conducts her own assessments:

You escort your prospective client into your office, which should be a comfortable, private space. Close the door to ensure privacy and prevent interruptions. If your office is in a high-traffic area or you have any other concerns about sound traveling, use a white noise machine to mask your conversation and drown out exterior sounds.

Introduce yourself to the client warmly to build up his comfort level, since many people feel nervous, apprehensive and vulnerable when meeting a mental health professional. This is especially true if it's their first-ever experience with counseling.

Allow your client to get settled in before you start asking questions. When he has gotten comfortable, start off with a general query such as, "So what brought you here today?" If you use a questionnaire that the client has filled out prior to the session, you can use it as a basis for your discussion. Otherwise, follow his lead and let him choose the topics.

As the client speaks, you will want to make brief notes of the important points while demonstrating that you are listening actively. This can be done by asking appropriate questions or simply punctuating the conversation with expressions like, "I see" or "I understand." Let the client know that you're taking notes to help you remember the highlights of your talk. When some clients see you writing, they're afraid that you're writing down judgments or documenting something because it's shocking. Explaining the true purpose helps alleviate this fear.

Once the client has shared his issue and any other relevant information, you can explain in general terms how you would approach the situation. Many people don't know exactly how therapy works. They might believe that you're there to give them specific advice, or on the flipside that you're simply there to listen. Give the client an overview of your therapeutic approach, and also explain your schedule, fees and other logistical information.

At this time, you should also discuss privacy, the circumstances in which you would have to break confidentiality, and other matters that are covered by informed consent. If you have pre-printed information, give a copy to the client and go over it carefully, answering any questions he might have.

If the client is comfortable with this, he will choose to make another appointment and you'll continue to work together to build up a therapeutic relationship. Have him sign the informed consent forms so your next session can focus immediately on your work. The next time you meet, you can present a formal treatment plan and settle on the specific goals. If the client isn't comfortable, reassure him that it's okay and urge him to find a therapist with a more compatible style or approach.

A Day at a Social Service Agency

Working as a mental health counselor at a social service agency is a fairly common position in which you would deal with a diverse group of clients and issues. To get an idea of how a professional counselor might spend a typical day, we'll follow a mental health counselor named Amanda through her workday. This is a very general example; the specifics can vary widely out in the real world. Still, it will give you a flavor for what you might expect.

Amanda has a master's degree in psychology and is a licensed professional counselor. She works for a privately funded social service agency in its Community Counseling Program (CCP), where she has been employed for the last three years. The agency is located on the outskirts of Chicago, Illinois, and the CCP provides subsidized services to low-income residents in the surrounding neighborhoods.

Clients come to this program to address a variety of problems and concerns, from stress, anxiety and depression to relationship or family issues. They pay for their counseling sessions on a sliding scale, based on their income. Amanda also runs parenting and anger management groups as a part of her regular duties at the agency. These groups are offered by the CCP as a free service to the community.

Amanda's workday typically runs from 10 a.m. to 6 p.m. Monday through Friday. These hours allow her to meet with clients who cannot come in earlier due to their work schedules. They also work well for her because she is married, with a working spouse and two school-age children. Her later start time allows her to get them off to school, and her husband picks them up on his way home from work.

Occasionally she works later to fill in for other counselors who facilitate various educational and therapy groups at the agency. She sometimes works on the weekends if there is a special educational program or other event.

When she does this, she receives make-up time that she can use to leave earlier or come in later on a regular workday.

Although some employees at the agency are paid by the hour, Amanda is a salaried employee who receives a fixed amount each pay period. The agency also provides professional liability insurance under a blanket policy and she receives medical and dental benefits, two weeks of paid vacation each year, and twelve paid holidays. She is a member of the American Counseling Association, and the agency pays for half of her dues. She is responsible for paying her own license renewal fee to the state each year.

Amanda's first appointment is scheduled for 10:30 a.m., which gives her half an hour to get settled in and pull out the files of the clients she'll be seeing. Her first client of the day is Perry, a young man struggling with relationship issues.

Amanda has been seeing Perry on a weekly basis for the past month. Their main goal is to help him learn to draw boundaries with his girlfriend. He's also learning communication skills that he can use for conflict resolution, both in his relationship and at his workplace.

Amanda is primarily a cognitive counselor, so her approach focuses on empowerment and requires active participation by the client. At each session, she does a quick check-in with Perry to see how the previous week has gone. After this debriefing, they go over the homework that Amanda has typically assigned at their previous session. They talk about the issues and Perry receives his next homework assignment.

Amanda grabs Perry's file and meets him in the lobby, which is shared with two other mental health counselors. She ushers him into her office and turns on a white noise machine just outside the door before she closes it. Like many other social service agencies, which often run on a shoestring budget, quarters are cramped and space is at a premium. The white noise machine helps to ensure privacy for counseling sessions.

Perry takes a seat on the couch across from Amanda. He tells her that his week has gone well and that he was able to stop a fight with his girlfriend before it escalated by using healthy communications techniques. He proudly reports that they were able to resolve the issue in a calm manner.

Next they move on to Perry's homework, which was to practice active listening skills. This is what he used to redirect the fight with his girlfriend into a healthy discussion. He describes specifically how he used the skills, and Amanda helps him focus on what went right and where he might improve even further.

During the discussion, Perry reluctantly admits that he argued with his girlfriend again the next day and that it didn't go so well. Amanda doesn't judge or chide him. Instead, she guides him through a comparison of the fight with the healthy discussion. She helps him identify ways in which he could have redirected the fight so that it, too, could have had a better outcome.

As they chat, Amanda takes notes which she will use to fill out her paper-work later. The agency requires that counselors summarize each session in a report, briefly reviewing the main points, progress towards the established goals, and any goals that may have been added, changed, or deleted.

Their discussion reveals that Perry has trouble sticking to healthy com-munication skills when he overreacts to the issue he's fighting about. This overreaction is fed by leftover anger from previous disagreements. Amanda points out that he is giving the past power over his present and allowing it to interfere in his relationship.

To help him recognize when he is doing this, she teaches him to use an "emotion scale" of one to ten. When he feels his anger reaching the boiling point, she tells him to use the scale to rate exactly how angry he's feeling. Then she tells him to look at the situation objectively and decide where it should really rate on the scale. She explains that if he's have a "ten reaction" to a situation that should realistically only rate a four, six points of his anger are being fed by something outside.

When he catches himself doing this, she directs him to consciously set aside the extra anger and focus his energy on resolving the current issue. His home-work is to use the emotion scale over the next week to test his reaction when-ever he has a disagreement with his girlfriend. At the next session, they agree to discuss the results and focus on finding the source of the excess anger.

Counseling sessions at the agency run for 50 minutes rather than a full hour. Technically this is supposed to allow the counselor to finish up her paperwork before bringing in her next client. Realistically it never gives Amanda enough time to fill out her report. She files her notes in Perry's folder and puts it in her drawer to be dealt with later when she'll have enough time to expand her quick scribbles. She never leaves files out on her desk because of confidentiality concerns.

Her next client is already waiting in the lobby. This time she is working with Kate, a single mother of two who is struggling with depression. Kate is on antidepressant medication prescribed by a psychiatrist. The doctor felt that the underlying cause of her depression was situational rather than strictly chemical, so he referred her to the CCP for counseling.

Amanda has been working with Kate for two months. They start each visit by using the Beck Depression Inventory to assess the current severity of Kate's depression. One of their goals is to reduce her depression level as measured by the scale and to maintain the lowered score.

Amanda discovers that Kate's score today indicates mild-to-moderate depression. It's within one point of her score at their last session. Kate's homework was focused on teaching her how to avoid being a reactor to her depression symptoms. For example, when she was feeling tired and tempted to stay in bed or felt like isolating herself from others, Amanda taught her to ask herself, "Will this choice feed into my depression? If so, what can I do differently to combat the depression?"

Kate says that she was using the technique successfully in the beginning of the week, but then she got sick over the weekend. This caused her to start feeling sorry for herself, and she stopped using her cognitive tools and starting slipping back into her depressive symptoms.

Amanda helps her explore reasons why she might have allowed herself to slip. They discover that the illness allowed Kate to justify a lapse in her progress. She confesses that a part of her seems to be afraid of recovering from the depression.

For her homework, Amanda instructs her to journal about that fear. She gives Kate some questions to answer that are focused on getting to the root of the fear. At their next session, they will analyze Kate's writings for new insights.

Amanda sees two more clients before her lunch break. Because she starts work at 10, she doesn't go to lunch until 2:30. She gets a 30 minute lunch break. When she returns, she devotes an hour to catching up on her paperwork. At 4 p.m. she is scheduled to lead a parenting support group that meets at the agency twice a month.

The parenting group is open to anyone in the community who has at least one child under the age of 18. Its purpose is to give support to the group members and remind them that they're not alone. They share their parenting challenges with each other and seek opinions from the rest of the group. For the most part Amanda lets the conversation progress on its own, with group members finding answers and solutions through peer discussion. She only intervenes if someone tries to interrupt or cross-talk, if the group gets off topic, or if they seem to be headed in an unhealthy direction.

The group meets for 45 minutes, after which Amanda grabs a quick cup of coffee in the break room. Next up is a private supervision session with the staff psychologist. Each counselor in the CCP gets at least one hour of supervision each week. At these sessions, they summarize their current cases. The supervisor gives them feedback on what they're doing right and what might need to be changed. She also gives advice if needed.

These supervision sessions are the only time that Amanda ever discusses specifics of her cases with anyone. She occasionally has general discussions with colleagues, but she is careful not to share any identifying information in those talks. Clients give permission for the supervisory discussions by signing a consent form at the beginning of their treatment.

Amanda devotes the rest of the day to paperwork, returning phone calls and updating her schedule. She sees that one client has canceled for tomorrow, so she blocks out the time to prepare for a domestic violence awareness seminar that she'll be giving at the local high school next week. By the time 6 p.m. rolls around she has completed her progress notes and filed her client folders in a locked cabinet so she can head home with no outstanding paperwork waiting for her tomorrow.

Amanda's story presents a very general description of what a mental health counselor might do in a typical day. Counseling is just one part of an overall job that typically includes:

- Preparatory duties
- Providing direct service to individuals and/or groups
- Completing paperwork and other documentation
- Supervision sessions
- Appointment scheduling

The hours, duties, responsibilities, and pace of work might be very different in another specialty such as rehabilitation counseling, school counseling, or marriage and family therapy. They'll also differ based on your particular employer and whether there is any support staff. The main similarities lie in the fact that counseling is a helping profession. Whether you're in a social service agency, elementary school, government office or private clinic, your efforts will be focused on helping clients in some way. Although you might do it a little differently, the end result is still the same: giving guidance and teaching strategies so others can improve their lives.

CHAPTER SUMMARY

- Counselors can turn to peers for support with professional issues.
- Counselors use many tools, such as tests, assessment and treatment planners, to streamline their work.
- Professional organizations offer networking opportunities, publications, conferences, and other useful resources.
- At a first appointment, a counselor typically gathers information on a client's issue, gives an overview of how she would approach it, and discusses informed consent.
- A counselor's typical workday varies by specialty and workplace, but it always involves helping clients to improve their lives in some way.

"Oh, No, I Made a Mistake!"

Sometimes, even with the best planning and preparation, things don't work out the way you had hoped. You can research what it takes to prepare for a certain job, go through years of schooling, and even work your way through a practicum and internship that gives you a taste of on-the-job experience. Everything seems fine until you enter the working world. Then you wake up one day and say, "Oh, no, I made a mistake!"

This can happen early on, or you might put a few years into your counseling career and realize that you'd be miserable sticking with it for the long-term. The idea of going back to school and studying for another career is overwhelming, but so is the idea of sticking with a job you dislike. What do you do now?

DON'T GIVE UP TOO QUICKLY

Even when you love your work, there are bound to be days when you question the wisdom of your choice. It happens in just about every field, but it can be more pronounced in professional counseling because of the nature of the work. Counselors interact with their clients on a deep personal and emotional level. Even if you're good at maintaining barriers, there are times when the self-protective wall might crack. If this happens too often, you'll quickly be drained. You'll end up dreading your work because the personal cost has become too great.

When this happens, it's natural to consider giving up and finding a more peaceful profession. But the easy way out isn't always the best choice for the long term. Before you pack it in, make every effort to find out the specific causes of your stress and negative feelings and to see if there is some way to combat them. This process is very similar to how a cognitive counselor has her clients approach their own problems.

First, ask yourself, "Why, specifically, am I thinking about leaving the counseling profession?" Make a list of all the reasons. It will probably contain things like, "I'm stressed at the end of every day" or "I'm tired of dealing with unmotivated clients" or "It depresses me to hear everyone's problems all day." Don't judge yourself. Just write down everything that comes to your mind.

Next, for each of the reasons, ask yourself, "Have I done everything possible to fix this? If not, what else can I try?" For example, if your stress level is consistently high, have you tried strategies to reduce it? Do you do self-care activities like journaling, meditation, or even taking a nice, hot bubble bath? Have you asked your supervisor for her recommendations on how to detach more effectively?

Once you have identified new strategies, make a plan to implement them. Put it in writing so you have a neutral touchstone to which you can refer. When you're feeling stressed, frustrated or depressed, pull out the plan and ask yourself, "Am I following these steps?" If not, redirect yourself immediately.

If you've tried to take power over your negative feelings and they're still persisting, you may want to shift to another type of work within the counseling field. For example, if you're working in an outpatient substance abuse clinic and dealing mainly with court-ordered clients, their motivation is not likely to be high. If this frustrates you, you can try to detach from the feeling but it's probably going to crop up again. Perhaps you can move to vocational counseling, where clients tend to have higher motivation because they're initiating the work.

Or perhaps you're struggling in an overworked, understaffed government office. You enjoy your work, but the satisfaction is overshadowed by a too-heavy caseload and a lack of effective supervision. If you move to a group counseling practice, you can do the same kind of work but the conditions might be better.

If you can't come up with any ideas on your own, talk to your supervisor or a trusted colleague to see if they have any suggestions. You might even discover that they once struggled with doubts, too, and still made it through, so they can advise you from personal experience.

A WORLD OF OTHER OPTIONS

Sometimes, no matter how hard you try, you don't find a workable solution. Fortunately a master's degree in counseling is a very versatile tool that doesn't lock you into one set of career options. At its most basic, counseling psychology is focused on the study of people and how to work with them to achieve positive results. You learn specific therapeutic techniques, but you also learn valuable general skills that can be applied to a variety of jobs. These skills include:

- Listening and communication skills
- Empathy
- Objectivity
- Respect for diversity
- Interviewing and assessment skills
- Testing administration and interpretation
- Ability to guide and teach others
- Ability to help others find positive solutions
- Conflict resolution
- Ability to work with both individuals and groups

You also learn writing and organizational skills because they are required to make it successfully through your master's program even though they're not necessarily counseling skills.

Although your options are wide open, there are several fields where many of these skills are especially applicable. We'll look at them in a little more depth to give you an idea of your options.

Human Resources

In recent decades, the Personnel field has morphed into an incarnation called "Human Resources." This name is more accurate because it acknowledges the importance of the human element in contributing to an employer's success. People are indeed a resource, and those who work in H. R. must have the proper skills for dealing effectively with job applicants and employees.

Human resources professionals are responsible for screening, interviewing and hiring new employees. They are charged with the task of finding the right applicant for each particular job. They do this through resume and application screening, testing, and interviewing. Counselors learn how to administer tests and how to

> *At its most basic, counseling psychology is focused on the study of people and how to work with them to achieve positive results.*

assess people in face-to-face sessions. These skills can be translated into the human resources environment in employment-related positions.

Some human resources professionals have jobs through which they support employees who are currently working for the company. This may be done in a variety of ways. There are benefits administrators who help employees make decisions about their insurance and troubleshoot coverage problems. They offer empathy and help, and since they might be discussing a medical issue, they also maintain the employee's confidentiality. These are all skills that are learned in a counseling program.

The human resources department may also implement job satisfaction programs and other initiatives. Earning a counseling degree imparts the skills needed to identify workers' needs, find potential solutions, create and implement new programs, and measure their success. These tasks require interviewing skills and rapport building to get information from employees, problem-solving abilities to craft programs based on their input, and research and statistical knowledge to analyze the outcome.

Human resources professionals also handle the unpleasant task of carrying out terminations. A person might be fired because of their performance, or there might be a widespread layoff. Either way, it's never pleasant to tell someone that they no longer have a job. Counseling programs teach people to remain calm and objective even when confronted with intense emotion and to project empathy and understanding. This can be an invaluable skill when handling the prickly task of telling someone that they're losing their job.

According to Indeed.com, as of 2008 salaries in the human resources field ranged from an average of $47,000 for a human resources generalist to $60,000 for a specialist. This varies by experience and workplace.

Education and Training

You may think "education" only refers to teaching jobs at elementary schools, high schools, and colleges, but it goes far beyond that. Educators are found in a variety of settings, including the corporate world and government agencies. Companies need to train their workers and help them keep their skills up-to-date. They may do this through an internal training and development program, by sending their employees to on-site or off-site seminars conducted by an outside vendor, or a combination of both.

Your master's degree in counseling qualifies you for both school and corporate/government jobs. You may be able to teach psychology-related courses at the high school and/or college level, depending on your particular state's requirements. You can also develop, deliver and evaluate training programs for companies and government agencies. In those positions, you will work with adult learners and focus on job-specific skills. These might be concrete tasks such as operating machinery or using a particular type of software or "soft skills" like learning how to manage time or delegate work more effectively.

As a corporate or governmental trainer, you might be a direct employee or work for a training or consulting firm. While a job with a company or government agency may be more secure, consulting can offer higher pay, a more flexible schedule, and a wider variety of work.

If you opt to be a teacher, you can expect to earn an average of $49,000 according to Indeed.com. This applies to both the high school and college levels. Indeed.com says that corporate trainers were earning an average of $58,000 as of 2008.

Criminal Justice

A master's degree in counseling prepares you to deal with difficult people and those who are struggling with emotional issues. Both of these skills are invaluable for those who work in the criminal justice system.

Typical jobs in this category include police officer, corrections officer, and parole officer. These jobs have similarities, but each involves a different stage of the criminal justice process. As a member of the police force, you will deal with suspects at the point of apprehension. Corrections officers work in jails and prisons, interacting with suspects awaiting trial and those who have been convicted and are serving out their sentences. A parole officer deals with them once they completed their sentence and are being integrated back into society.

The therapeutic techniques, conflict resolution and active listening skills that you learned in your counseling program can be very useful in dealing with these populations. Many offenders are struggling with negative emotions such as anger and resentment. They see workers in the criminal justice system as their adversaries and respond accordingly. If you can handle them with empathy and respect, you can make a positive impact with some.

In any of these positions, you will frequently deal with unmotivated individuals who don't want to be helped, and some will be potentially violent. You must be able to detach, remain calm under pressure, and make quick decisions because the stakes can be very high. If you were disturbed by the risk of workplace violence when you were a counselor, or if you had difficulty detaching, criminal justice may not be a good alternate field.

Salaries in this field vary, depending on the particular job you choose. According to Indeed.com, in 2008 police officers were earning an average yearly salary of $46,000, while parole officers earned $39,000 and correctional officers earned $34,000.

Management/Supervision

Supervisors and managers are charged with the responsibility of getting work done through their work team. Like counselors, they deal directly with people, giving them work assignments and guiding them to the achievement of goals. Because these goals are work related, a supervisor or manager must also ensure that her employees are doing their jobs effectively and institute corrective action when they're not. Just as in counseling, this requires the ability to communicate effectively with people, detach from negative responses, remain objective and goal focused, and promote teamwork and healthy conflict resolution.

Supervisors and managers can be found in every department of virtually any workplace. Some companies hire personnel at the supervisory level, while others prefer to promote from within. For the latter, you will need to take an entry-level position and earn experience and seniority in order to gain a promotion to management.

Because of the wide range of supervisory positions, typical salaries vary widely too. According to Indeed.com, as of 2008 annual supervisory wages ranged from $32,000 on up, with an overall average of $54,000.

Market Research

A large part of counseling is learning how to assess people and to read their feelings. A master's degree in counseling typically covers administering tests, conducting research, and analyzing the results. All of these skills can be valuable assets in the market research field.

Many research firms recruit participants and conduct surveys, interviews, and focus groups. This may be done to aid in the development of new products, test consumer opinions about new and existing products, test the effectiveness of an advertising campaign, gauge consumer spending habits, or for a host of other reasons. A degree in counseling gives you experience in testing, assessment, and working with individual and groups that can be directly applied to market research projects.

Besides interacting directly with people, you may be qualified to design studies. This might include developing questionnaires and activities, deciding on the correct demographic profile for study participants, deciding how they will be recruited, and spelling out exactly how the study will be conducted and how the data will be analyzed.

Salaries in this field can vary widely, depending on your employer, position and experience. According to Indeed.com, as of 2008 a senior market research analyst could earn up to $75,000.

Sales

When you earn a master's degree in counseling, much of your work revolves around understanding people and their motivations and learning how to guide and influence them. These are all skills that can be used by a professional salesperson too.

If you've ever watched an expert car salesman, you'll notice that he uses a heavy dose of psychology. He'll greet potential customers in a warm and friendly manner, setting up the groundwork for a positive relationship. He'll use questions to subtly assess them, figuring out just how serious they are and the price range they can likely afford. He'll build rapport by finding and emphasizing common ground, from being a fellow parent to rooting for the same sports team. He'll get them in a positive frame of mind by asking questions that would logically be answered with a "yes" so they're more likely to answer affirmatively when discussing a purchase.

Most successful salespeople have little or no formal training in psychology. They possess a natural talent that gets honed on the job. If you already have a counseling degree, you'll be able to skip much of the learning curve and achieve success more quickly.

While retail salespeople are the most well known because they're highly visible, you can get a job selling virtually anything, from business equipment to pharmaceuticals. Your potential customers might be consumers, professionals in a particular field, or corporate purchasing departments.

Sales is often a high pressure job. In many positions, the largest chunk of your income comes from commissions so you won't earn much if you don't perform well. Your manager might ride herd and continually press you to increase your numbers, and you may be in cut-throat competition with your co-workers. If counseling was too stressful, sales might not be the right alternate career choice.

While the average overall earnings for sales positions is $49,000 according to Indeed.com, earning potential in this field is often limited only by your own efforts, motivation and skill. Many salespeople earn a small base salary and make the bulk of their money through commissions.

COMBINING PERSONAL INTERESTS WITH WORK

Sometimes you can blend a personal interest or hobby with your counseling degree and turn it into a new career. Counseling skills fit well in a variety of other fields like the ones discussed below.

Fitness/Personal Training

Perhaps you are a fitness buff who jogs for miles or hits the gym every day. You may be able to combine that passion with your counseling degree to help others maintain motivation and achieve their own fitness goals. You can become a personal trainer, and you'll have more to offer than most. You'll understand the psychological components that make the difference between success and failure for someone who is working on a fitness routine.

This particular field will take some additional training, as you'll want to earn professional certification as a personal trainer. Don't worry, the process won't take nearly as long as earning your master's degree and it will only be a fraction of the cost.

The three biggest organizations offering certification for personal trainings are the American Council on Exercise (ACE), the American College of Sports Medicine (ACSM) and the National Academy of Sports Medicine (NASM) but there are others that may offer their own programs. Typically you can complete your training within a few months, followed by successfully passing an exam to earn your certification. The cost of study materials can be several hundred dollars, and the exam itself can cost up to $250.

Once you receive your certification, you can offer personal training services that incorporate sports psychology principles. Just as you would develop a treatment plan with a counseling client that addresses emotional challenges and barriers, you can do the same with fitness clients. This gives them an extra tool to use in achieving their physical goals because they'll also be able to knock down their inner barriers.

According to Indeed.com, the average salary for a certified personal trainer was $32,000 in 2008. This amount varies by employment location and hours worked, since the amount of clients you will have at any particular time can vary widely.

FREELANCE WRITING

You probably completed a lot of papers in the course of earning your master's degree. If you've always enjoyed writing and have a knack for it, or if you developed an affinity for it during your college years, you might be able to parlay that into a new career.

Many self-help and general interest magazines publish articles with a psychological slant. People are always interested in learning how to improve themselves, especially if the information is presented in a simple, step-by-step format. You can write pieces on any common problem, from stress management to overcoming phobias to learning how to say no. Women's magazines are always looking for good relationship advice, so if you have experience in couples counseling this may be a lucrative niche.

You may also want to consider writing self-help books. Marketdata, a research firm, estimated that the American self-improvement market was over $11 billion in 2008. This figure includes everything from infomercials to instructional CDs and DVDs, but books do account for a significant chunk.

Your counseling degree qualifies you to write knowledgeably on a variety of self-help topics. If you're creative and can put a unique spin on common-sense advice, you may find success as an author.

The freelance writing field is highly competitive, and rejection is a way of life. You must be able to toughen your skin and keep submitting, no matter how thick your stack of rejection slips grows. If you left the counseling field because you were discouraged by a lack of success, this might not be the best career alternate for you. However, you may be able to use it to supplement your income while working another job.

Magazine writers are typically paid by the word, although many publications offer a flat fee for articles. This can run anywhere from $100 for regional publications to $1000 or more for magazines sold on national newsstands. For books, the writer receives royalties based on sales, and the publisher may give an advance on that amount.

Personal Insight

FROM THE AUTHOR: Even though I enjoy my counseling work, I've always loved writing and I often meld it with my professional knowledge. I write self-help articles for a variety of magazines, and I enjoy this supplemental work because I can gear it to my personal interests. For example, I often write about parenting topics or how to supervise employees effectively because I have professional experience with both of those subjects. I also am an animal lover, so I've done several articles on how your actions and emotions can affect your pet. I've expanded into writing books, as you might have guessed since you're holding an example in your hands right now.

It is hard to make a living through freelance writing alone, but if you like to write and want to supplement your income, it can be an excellent sideline. It's also a good way to earn money if you're between jobs or if you need a flexible schedule.

OTHER OPTIONS

The list of potential jobs in this chapter is not meant to be all-inclusive. It gives a quick overview of some of the fields that are open to people with a master's degree in counseling, but there are many more. Virtually any professional whose focus involves dealing directly with people or helping them in some way might be appropriate. This can include anything from public relations to customer service. Your options are limited only by your imagination; if you can think of a way to weave psychological concepts into a job, it's a likely candidate.

A COMPLETE CAREER CHANGE

Sometimes you may need a complete shift of career. You discover that you simply don't want to work in any field that resembles professional counseling in any way. If this happens, don't judge yourself. Everyone makes bad decisions from time to time. It's frustrating when the decision includes years of study and considerable expense, but you're powerless to change that. Beating yourself up wastes precious energy that could be focused towards the future.

Once you find a new job in an entirely different field, you might want to work counseling into your life in a way that you can control. By doing volunteer work, you can set your own terms and avoid feeling trapped and frustrated. Social service agencies, domestic violence shelters, and other community-based programs welcome volunteer counselors with open arms.

If you'd like to meld your work with spirituality, see if your church has a Stephen Ministry program. Stephen Ministry is a non-denominational program that trains caregivers to use empathy and active listening skills so they can provide Christian-based support to people with emotional needs.

Although most Stephen Ministers are lay people without any formal training other than what is provided by the program, counselors are welcome as long as they are willing to work within the established boundaries. Stephen Ministers don't "treat" their care receivers. Instead, they listen and offer support.

CHAPTER SUMMARY

- No matter how closely you weigh your decision to become a counselor, sometimes you'll discover that you made a mistake.
- Before you decide to leave the professional counseling field, you should examine your reasons and see if you can create a plan to neutralize them.
- You may be able to get good advice from your supervisor or a trusted colleague.
- Even if you decide to leave the profession, your counseling degree has prepared you for a number of other fields. These might include human resources, education/training, criminal justice, management/supervision, market research, and sales.
- You may be able to combine your new job with a personal interest such as physical fitness or writing.
- Even if you don't want to have a career that resembles professional counseling in any way, you may be able to use those skills on a volunteer basis.

Conclusion

There's a tale about an old gentleman who goes for a walk on the beach at sunrise. He spots a young boy walking down the shore line, picking up starfish and flinging them into the water. He asks, "What are you doing?" and the boy explains that the starfish will die if they're left on the sand in the morning sun.

The old man shakes his head. "But the beach goes on for miles," he says, "and there must be hundreds of starfish. You'll never be able to save them all. What difference can your efforts possibly make?"

The boy glances down at the starfish in his hand before tossing it to safety in the waves. "It makes a different to this one," he says.

(Inspired by The Star Thrower by Loren Eiseley.)

If you choose a career in professional counseling, you're embarking on a long, hard journey. First you'll have to invest several years of education. Then you'll have to gain experience and make it through the licensure process. Once you get through all that, you'll focus on a job that has no guaranteed outcome. You'll do your best to help people change their lives for the better. Some will manage to do so, but many others will falter and back away. Over time, the failures can be disheartening and start to overshadow the successes.

When that happens, remind yourself of the starfish story. By entering a caring profession, you've shown your desire and commitment to helping others. You can't "save" every client, but every time you show someone how to make healthy changes in his life or guide him through the minefield of a difficult decision or help him emerge from the dark tunnel of depression, you've made a difference to that one.

That's what counseling is all about.

Resources

For the latest updates to these resources and other information contained in this book, or to ask the author a question, visit the So You Want To Be A Counselor blog at http://counselorwannabe.blogspot.com. You can email the author directly at counselorwannabe@gmail.com.

PROFESSIONAL ORGANIZATIONS

As a mental health counselor, you can take advantage of a wide variety of networking, support and professional development opportunities. No matter which field or specialty you choose, there will likely be an organization or association geared to your interests. Many are not-for-profit associations, and they typically offer informational resources, support, training opportunities, networking, job information and leads, and publications such as newsletters, magazines and journals. If you're a student, you may be eligible for a discounted membership. Even if you don't join, you may find useful information on their websites.

The following list includes a wide sampling of professional organizations, but it's not all-inclusive. You can find others through internet searches or recommendations from instructors and colleagues.

- American Academy of Grief Counseling (AAGC), www.aihcp.org/aagc.htm
- American Association of Christian Counselors (AACC), www.aacc.net
- American Association of Pastoral Counselors (AAPC), www.aapc.org
- American Board of Christian Sex Therapists, www.sexualwholeness.com/abcst/index.htm
- American College Counseling Association (ACCA), www.collegecounseling.org
- American Counseling Association (ACA), www.counseling.org
- American Rehabilitation Counseling Association (ARCA), www.arcaweb.org
- American School Counselor Association (ASCA), www.schoolcounselor.org

- American Mental Health Counselors Association (AHMCA), www.amhca.org
- Asian American Psychological Association (AAPA), www.aapaonline.org
- Association for Lesbian, Gay, Bisexual and Transgender Issues in Counseling, www.algbtic.org
- Association for Specialists in Group Work (ASGW), www.asgw.org
- Black African-American Christian Counselors (BAACC), www.aacc.net/divisions/baacc
- Association for Behavioral and Cognitive Therapies (ABCT), www.aabt.org
- International Association of Addiction and Offenders Counselors, www.iaaoc.org
- International Society for Mental Health Online (ISMHO), www.ismho.org
- National Association for Alcoholism and Drug Abuse Counselors (NAADAC), http://naadac.org
- National Association for College Admission Counseling (NACAC), www.nacacnet.org
- National Association of Adoption Counselors (NANC). www.nationalassociationofadoptioncounselors.org
- National Rehabilitation Counseling Association (NRCA), http://nrca-net.org

QUALITY ASSURANCE ORGANIZATIONS

This section lists organizations that offer credentials and certification for mental health professions and specialties. These organizations promote and maintain quality through their certification requirements.
- American Nurses Credentialing Center (ANCC), www.nursecredentialing.org
- Art Therapy Credentials Board (ATCB), www.atcb.org/registration_atr/
- Certification Board for Music Therapists (CBMT), www.cbmt.org/default.asp?page=FAQ
- Association for Counselor Education and Supervision, www.acesonline.net
- National Federation for Biblio/Poetry Therapy, www.nfbpt.com
- National Board for Certified Counselors (NBCC), www.nbcc.org

ASSOCIATIONS FOR RELATED CAREERS

This section lists organizations and associations that cover professional options beyond mental health counseling. Some are general, while others are aimed at a specific group of professionals within a particular field.

- American Art Therapy Association (AATA), www.arttherapy.org
- American Dance Therapy Association (ADTA), www.adta.org
- American Association of Pastoral Counselors (AAPC), www.aapc.org
- American Psychiatric Association (APA), www.psych.org
- American Psychiatric Nurses Association (APNA), www.apna.org
- American Psychological Association (APA), www.apa.org

- Association for Play Therapy, www.a4pt.org
- Association of Black Psychologists (ABP), www.abpsi.org
- Certified Coaches Federation (CCF) , www.certifiedcoachesfederation.com
- European Coaching Institute (ECI), www.europeancoachinginstitute.org
- International Association of Coaching (IAC), www.certifiedcoach.org
- International Coaching Council (ICC), www.international-coaching-council.com
- International Coach Federation (ICF),www.coachfederation.org
- International Guild of Coaches (IGC), www.lifecoachguild.org
- National Association for Drama Therapy (NADT), www.nadt.org
- National Association for Poetry Therapy (NAPT), www.poetrytherapy.org
- National Association of Black Social Workers (NABSW), www.nabsw.org/mserver
- National Association of Social Workers (NASW), www.naswdc.org
- New England Association of Holistic Counselors (NEHCA), www.nehcaweb.org.

ACCREDITATION AGENCIES

This section includes organizations that offer accreditation for schools and educational programs.

- American Association of Colleges of Nursing (AACN), www.aacn.nche.edu
- Council for Accreditation of Counseling and Related Educational Programs (CACREP), www.cacrep.org
- Council for Higher Education Accreditation (CHEA), www.chea.org
- Distance Education and Training Council (DETC), www.detc.org
- Middle States Association of Schools and Colleges (MSA) accredits schools in Delaware, the District of Columbia, Maryland, New Jersey, New York, and Pennsylvania. Website: www.middlestates.org
- National League for Nursing (NLN), www.nln.org
- The New England Association of Schools and Colleges (NEASC) accredits schools in Connecticut, Maine, Massachusetts, New Hampshire, Rhode Island, and Vermont. Website: www.neasc.org
- The North Central Association Commission on Accreditation and School Improvement (NCA) accredits schools in Arizona, Arkansas, Colorado, Illinois, Indiana, Iowa, Kansas, Michigan, Minnesota, Missouri, Navajo Nation, Nebraska, New Mexico, North Dakota, Ohio, Oklahoma, South Dakota, West Virginia, Wisconsin, and Wyoming. Website: www.ncacasi.org.
- The Northwest Association of Schools and Colleges (NWCCU) accredits schools in Alaska, Idaho, Montana, Nevada, Oregon, Utah, and Washington State. Website: www.nwccu.org
- The Southern Association of Schools and Colleges (SACS) accredits schools in Alabama, Florida, Georgia, Kentucky, Louisiana, Mississippi, North Caro-

lina, South Carolina, Tennessee, Texas and Virginia. Website: www.sacs.org
- The Western Association of Schools and Colleges (WASC) accredits schools in California and Hawaii. Website: www.wascweb.org
- The United States Department of Education (USDE), www.ed.gov/admins/finaid/accred/index.html

ETHICAL CODES

These websites contain codes of ethics for various organizations for mental health professions and related fields.

- American Association for Marriage and Family Therapy code of ethics, www.aamft.org/resources/LRM_Plan/Ethics/ethicscode2001.asp
- American Association of Christian Counselors code of ethics, www.aacc.net/about-us/code-of-ethics/
- American Association of Pastoral Counselors code of ethics, www.aapc.org/content/ethics
- American Association of Sexuality Educators, Counselors and Therapists code of ethics, www.aasect.org/codeofethics.asp
- American Counseling Association ethics and professional standards, www.counseling.org/Resources/CodeOfEthics/TP/Home/CT2.aspx
- American Mental Health Counselors Association code of ethics, www.amhca.org/code/
- American Music Therapy Association code of ethics, www.musictherapy.org/ethics.html
- American School Counselor Association ethical standards, www.schoolcounselor.org/content.asp?contentid=173
- Association for Comprehensive Energy Psychology code of ethics, http://energypsych.org/displaycommon.cfm?an=1&subarticlenbr=1
- Association for Specialists in Group Work professional standards, www.asgw.org/training_standards.htm
- Commission on Rehabilitation Counselor Certification code of ethics, www.crccertification.com/pages/code_of_ethics/10.php
- Feminist Therapy Institute code of ethics, www.feminist-therapy-institute.org/ethics.htm
- National Association of Social Workers code of ethics, www.socialworkers.org/pubs/code/default.asp
- National Board for Certified Counselors code of ethics, www.nbcc.org/AssetManagerFiles/ethics/nbcc-codeofethics.pdf
- National Board for Certified Counselors internet counseling code of ethics, www.nbcc.org/AssetManagerFiles/ethics/internetCounseling.pdf
- National Federation for Biblio/Poetry Therapy code of ethics, www.nfbpt.com/codeofethics.html

FINANCIAL AID RESOURCES

These websites will help you find financial aid for college and gain more information about this topic.

- College Scholarships search site, www.collegescholarships.org
- Collegeboard.com scholarship search database, http://apps.college-board.com/cbsearch_ss/welcome.jsp
- FastWeb scholarship information and search, www.fastweb.com/
- FinAid tuition calculator, www.finaid.org/calculators/costprojector.phtml
- Free Application for Federal Student Aid (FAFSA), www.fafsa.ed.gov
- National Consumer Law Center's Student Loan Borrower Assistance, www.studentloanborrowerassistance.org

CURRENT JOB OUTLOOK AND SALARY INFORMATION

These websites provide information on current salary prospects and job availability for mental health counselors and related professions.

- U. S. Department of Labor Bureau of Labor Statistics, www.bls.gov/oco/ocos067.htm
- Indeed.com salary search by job title and location, www.indeed.com/salary
- Salary.com cost of living information for the United States and major cities,http://swz.salary.com/CostOfLivingWizard/layouthtmls/coll_statebrief_A.html
- SimplyHired.com salary search, www.simplyhired.com/a/salary/search/q-counselor
- Yahoo HotJobs salary search, http://hotjobs.yahoo.com/salary

JOB SEARCH WEBSITES

Craigslist, www.craigslist.com
Federal government jobs, www.usajobs.gov
Indeed Job Search, www.indeed.com
Jobs.com, www.jobs.com
Monster, www.monster.com
SimplyHired, www.simplyhired.com
State government jobs, www.usa.gov/Agencies/State_and_Territories.shtml

References

Benshoff, J. (1993). Peer supervision in counselor training, Clinical Supervisor, 11(2), 89-102.

Carlbring, P., Ekselius, L., & Andersson, G. (2003). Treatment of panic disorder via the Internet: A randomized trial of CBT vs. applied relaxation. Journal of Behavior Therapy and Experimental Psychiatry, 34, 129-140.

Christensen, H., Griffiths, K. M., & Jorm, A. F. (2004). Delivering interventions for depression by using the Internet: Randomised controlled trial. British Medical Journal, 328, 265-268.

Christensen, H., Griffiths, K. M., & Korten, A. (2002). Web-based cognitive behavior therapy: Analysis of site usage and changes in depression and anxiety scores. Journal of Medical Internet Research, 4, 3.

Cook, J. E., & Doyle, C. (2002). Working alliance in online therapy as compared to face-to-face therapy: Preliminary results. CyberPsychology & Behavior, 5, 95-105.

Gatley, L. & Stabb, S. (2005). Psychology Students' Training in the Management of Potentially Violent Clients. Professional Psychology: Research and Practice, 36(6), 681-687.

Green, M., McInerney, A., Biesecker, B., & Fost, N. (2001). Education about genetic testing for breast cancer susceptibility: Patient preferences for a computer program or genetic counselor. American Journal of Medical Genetics, 103(1), 24-31.

Guy, J. D., Brown, C. K., & Polestra, P. L. (1990). Who gets attacked? A national survery of patient violence directed at psychologists in clinical practice. Professional Psychology: Research and Practice, 21, 493-495.

Lange, A., Rietdijk, & D., Hudcovicova, M. (2003). Interapy: A controlled randomized trial of the standardized treatment of posttraumatic stress through the internet. Journal of Consulting and Clinical Psychology, 71, 901-909.

Littlechild, B. (1995). Violence against social workers. Journal of Interpersonal Violence, 10, 123-131.

McAdams, C., & Foster, V. (2002). An assessment of resources for counselor coping and recovery in the aftermath of client suicide. Journal of Humanistic Counseling, Education and Development, 41(2), 232-241.

McAdams, C., & Foster, V. (2000). Client suicide: Its frequency and impact on counselors. Journal of Mental Health Counseling, 22, 107-121.

McPherson, M., Smith-Lovin, L., & Brashears, M. (2006). Social isolation in American: Changes in core discussion networks over two decades. American Sociological Review, 71(3), 353-375.

Montgomery, L., Cupit, B., & Wimberley, T. (1999). Complaints, malpractice, and risk management: Professional issues and personal experiences. Professional Psychology: Research and Practice, 30(4), 402-410.

Moscovitch, A., Chaimowitz, G. & Patterson, P. (1990). Trainee safety in psychiatric units and facilities. Canadian Journal of Psychiatry, 35, 634-635.

Nayak, S., Wheeler, B., Shiflett, S., & Agostinelli, S. (2000). Effect of music therapy on mood and social interaction among individuals with acute traumatic brain injury and stroke. Rehabilitation Psychology, 45(3), 274-283.

Newport, F. (2007). Just why do Americans attend church. Retrieved from www.gallup.com/poll/27124/Just-Why-Americans-Attend-Church.aspx.

Shaw, H. & Shaw, S. (2006). Critical ethics in online counseling: Assessing current practices with an ethical intent checklist, Journal of Counseling and Development, 84(1), 41-53.